To Bruce ?

What a delight to know you and your family and to know how you have ministered to our wonderful Lord.

Pastor Billy John Abney

i

The Power

of

DEBAR/REMA:

the Words of Faith!

"A study that will change your Life !"

Billy Yochanan Abney

The Power

of

debar/rhema :

the Words of Faith!

ACKNOWLEDGEMENTS

To Bryant Abney who taught me to work and to do the job right the first time, "Thanks Dad."

To Alice Abney who was the greatest teacher that I ever had, she taught by word and deed. "Thanks Mom."

To Pleasant Valley South Baptist Church in Floyd County, Georgia, where I started attending in 1930; where my parents served and ministered until their Homegoing.

To Mrs. Lamar Jackson who told me in 1954, that her son in the 6th grade had more education than I did but you can do it Mr. Abney. Thank you Mrs. Jackson.

To Mercer University who accepted me because I was an ordained minister even though I was not prepared for college. This was a policy that Jesse Mercer demanded. Thank you Dr. Mercer.

ACKNOWLEGEMENTS CONTINUED . . .

To Miss Bates who taught speed reading. She flashed a light on the board and asked what did we see? I saw a light, some saw a word. She said you are not training your mind to see what your eyes see. She gave a test and I was reading 90 words a minute, only comprehending 45% of what I was reading. After three months I was retested and was reading 250 words per minute and comprehending 90% of what I was reading. This opened up a world of knowledge in the Bible/ books to me. Thank you Miss Bates.

To Ruby Nell Erwin Abney my wife whose love made me more of a man than I thought I could be and all that I accomplished I owe to God and to her. Thank you, Lord, and Ruby Nell.

To Macedonia Church and Pastor Eddie Smith who whole heartedly accepted me in 1993, thank you Pastor and Mrs. Martha.

ACKNOWLEGEMENTS CONTINUED . . .

To Annie Ruth Taylor Land Abney who helped restore me emotionally and physically with her love. Thank you, Ann.

To Beth Yeshua and Rabbi Greg Hershberg for teaching me the Hebrew roots of the New Testament for 15 years, thank you Rabbi Greg and Bernadette.

To Elizabeth Park Tuten Faulk Abney who helped me to see the value of prophecy and shared prophecy with me for 7 years, what a glorious time this was. Thank you, Betty.

To Awakening Fires, Jason Thomley and Todd Hunt for fulfilling the vision of Betty and the fellowship of the family to Betty and me; thank you Jason and Todd.

To Dr. Lennie and Mrs. Marie Abney Poon for your faith and encouragement; without which this book would not have been written. Thanks, Doc and Marie.

ACKNOWLEGEMENTS CONTINUED . . .

To Nora Ruth my daughter who helped me prepare the manuscript to present to the editor and helped me with the editor's suggestions. Thank you, Nora Ruth.

To Dr. Ben Chandler, the editor who made many valuable suggestions and helped with clarification throughout the book.. He was God sent at a time when I had exhausted other publishing possibilities. Thank you, Dr. Ben for your help in designing the format, creating the book cover and preparing the manuscript for publication.

To God be all the glory, hallelujah!

DEDICATION

This book is dedicated to

William Bryant and Julia Alice Mathis Abney, and

To all their children and offspring.

To Ruby Nell Erwin Abney,

And our children in whom we became one.

Billy John, Jr., Julia Grace, Sara Virginia,

Bryant Erwin, Luther Dale, David Ralph and Nora Ruth

The purpose for writing this book

The Power of the Debar/Rema Word of Faith is to share with you what I have been able to glean on my journey from the books and minds of four men.

The journey started in September of 1963, when I took a course in seminary under Dr. Dale Moody, on *The Doctrine of the Holy Spirit.* He was researching the doctrine of the Holy Spirit and later published his book *The Spirit of the Living God* in 1968, Broadman Press, Nashville, Tennessee.

Dr. Moody referred in his book (The Word of Truth) on page 331, footnote 37, to an article on the new chronology of Paul's letters. In this new chronology he referred to two Oxford scholars. The first was C.F. Turner, in 1898, who stated that there are six (6) panels in the book of Acts 2. The second man was C.J. Cadoux, who expanded this [concept] of Turners in 1918, and dated the first panel in Acts as 30 AD.

Someone asked me how long it took me to develop the outline *A Holy Spirit Guide to Reading and Studying the New Testament* [see Addendum] and I replied about 40 years. But then I realized that I did not develop it, I just compiled it from studying the three men above.

I also used Dr. A. T. Robertson's, *Word Pictures of the New Testament,* in Volume 4, to get the outline of the Pauline Epistles. From these four men, I compiled and combined this outline as part of my journey of faith.

I pray that this book and the outline will help you on your journey of faith and, that you will have a happy voyage on your journey.

I met Dr. Ben Chandler on a voyage on the Grand Celebration (1-17-17) and it was a divine appointment by Adonai YHWH for me.

He has edited and corrected many jumbled up sentences and added his own thoughts and made this book readable, printable and understandable.

"*Telle lege;* (Take it, read it) and study the greatest book of all books, ***The Holy Bible.*** [1] I pray that your journey/voyage is a Bon Voyage!

---

1. Holiness, by JC Ryle; Stated in the Preface by J.I. Packer; Evangelical Press; 16/18;
    Welwyn, Hertfordshire, England

INTRODUCTION

You are reading a theology of the "Word of Faith" which has been and is being preached to the whole world by those called to proclaim God's Truth. In Hebrew it is *"debarim"* and in Greek the word is *"remata"* or "[the Word of Faith] which we are preaching to you" (Romans 10:8 TLV) "But what does it say? 'The word is near you, in your mouth and in your heart, that is, the word of faith that we are proclaiming' "which the Apostle Paul quoted from Deuteronomy 30:14.

The living [Oracles Acts 7:38c: "He received living words to pass on to us."] Debar/Rema Words of the living [Adonai, the Creator and Yah the Revealer/Redeemer], hereafter referred to as A/Y, is used six times in Psalms 118:5, 14; 17-19.

These living words fulfill what Jesus said in John 10:10b: "I have come that they might have life, and have it abundantly!" This book is written to help all unbelievers to receive the gift of eternal life and all believers to receive ABUNDANT life in Christ.

Contents

The Power

of

debar/rhema :

the Words of Faith!

CHAPTER 1

In 1983 I was talking to my son David about a course he took in college
and the text book he used in that course. The book was written by
Dr. Gerhard Von Rad, *The Message of the Prophets*.   (END) 1
I borrowed his book and devoured it. I was so excited about what I
read that I bought him a new book.

Dr. Von Rad, wrote in his book, "The term,
'the Word of Yahweh', occurs 241 times in
the Old Testament writings; of these no less
than 221 (92 percent) relate to a Prophetic
oracle." When I saw this I wanted to know
what that "Word of Yahweh" was! How was
it related to me as a servant (Doulos, Greek)
of Messiah (Christ) (Galatians 1:10) today?

> *In Hebrew it is*
> *"debarim" and in*
> *Greek the word is*
> *"remata" or*
>
> *["the Word of*
> *Faith"]*

Dr. Emil Brunner (END) 2   writes, "Nowhere is there one 'word' which
is the clue to the whole, a 'word' which unites all these varied ideas and
experiences. God reveals Himself through theophanies, angels,
dreams, oracles, and above all through the mysterious inspired 'word'

of the Prophets." These Debarim/Remata are the "**<u>mysterious inspired 'Word' of the Prophets</u>**," And, these are the clue to understanding the whole Old Testament and New Testament theological/revelation.

The first thing that I found was that the Word was *"DeBar."* I found this in Keil and Delitzsch, commentary:

> *"From Zion there would go forth Torah, i.e, instruction as to the questions which man has to put to God, and from Jerusalem the Word **[DeBar]** of Jehovah by which He created the world at first, and by which it is **[we are]** spiritually created anew." [Hebrews 1:3]* (END) 3 I was blown away.

I began a search to find out how the scholars of the Old Testament dealt with these words. I was surprised when I discovered that most did not deal with them at all, and in my reading I went on a treasure hunt because I knew that something had been left out of most Old Testament writings that was **<u>very</u> important**. This search has lasted for thirty years, and when I discovered some mention of the term I was elated.

Even until this day, the Words have not been discussed as they **<u>must be.</u>** James F.G. Dunn says, "Did the First Christians Worship Jesus?" (END) 4 Contemporary linguistic philosophers would speak of God's Speech/ Act [Act/Event] of (DeBarim).

I found this confirmed in the Book of Hebrews of the New Testament (NT here after) paraphrased: "Bearing [Upholding] all things by the (Remata) Word of His Power." The Tree of Life Version says: *"This Son*

[Jesus Christ – bold added] *is the radiance of His glory and the imprint of His being, upholding all things by His powerful word."* [Hebrews 1:3]

I knew that I had struck something more wonderful than gold for the soul, and by Dr. A.T. Robertson, (END) 5, in his discussion of Acts 5:32 which says:

> **"And we are witnesses of these events (things /rhematon)." [Literally, "sayings", but like the Hebrew "dabher" for 'word' it is here used for "things."] - as is the Rusch ha –Kodesh, whom God has given to those who obey Him."**

I had never asked in forty-five (45) years of quoting this passage what "these things" were. When I did, I received a great shock.

The Holy Spirit does not bear witness to "things," but He bears witness to the Debar/Remata Words of A/Y. Acts 5:31 [TLV] says, *"This One God exalted at His right hand as Leader and Savior, to give repentance to Israel and removal of sins."*

How about that! This shows how many different ways these words are translated in OT/NT or rather mistranslated.

Again, Von Rad says:

> *"It is very significant that the phrase always appears with the definite article, 'the Word of Yahweh', and never in the indefinite form , 'a word of Yahveh', as a superficial glance at the extremely large number of such 'word events' might have led one to expect."* (END) 6

Brown-Driver-Briggs says in their *Hebrew/English Lexicon,*   (END) 7 that "**Word of God**, as a divine communication in the form of commandments, prophecy, and Words of help to His People, [is] used 394 times." This shows why the search can never stop; because new knowledge is being discovered all the time. This is quite an increase from 241 times to 394.

This is what amazed me! Just to see how many times that the DeBarim was used in the OT and to find that they had <u>not</u> been discussed by the large majority of the OT Scholars was amazing. Von Rad/ Dunn translated the DeBar as "Word Event." When I saw this translation I was getting more excited by the moment!

In K&D I found a statement which blew me away, and it was: "DeBar of Yahve are words of the false Prophets, with which they give out that their prophesyings [as] God's word." (END) 8 I said how can that be? They may use these words that way when they are prophesying falsely, but not as they are used in all the OT books. Von Rad/ Dunn' refutes this statement.

I was discouraged, and I knew that I did not have the time or the ability to refute this argument or statement. So, I gave Von Rad's book away to a young man. Again, I thought my thirty year search had ended without me being able to find the <u>uses</u> and <u>meaning</u> of these great Debars.

On March 17, 2013, my sister had surgery on her broken leg in Cummings, Georgia. My niece and her husband were at the hospital, and she asked me how things were going with the book, and I was telling her. She said, "Uncle Billy you have got to write down what you know about the DeBars/Rema Words." Her words, spoken by the Holy

Spirit, were words of inspiration to me, which lit a fire in my soul and renewed me to keep searching for the correct translation and interpretation of these words.

On March 19 or 21, 2013, I was reading my former Professor's, [Dr. Dale Moody] book which I had read many times before, but this was the *kairos* ["the fullness of time" See: Galatians 4:4] time, and he says, "The most basic meaning is the prophetic word of God summed up in 2 Peter 1:19, in the apostolic declaration that 'we have the prophetic word made more sure.' This Old Testament meaning of the Word [DeBar] of God is profound," (END) 9 and, he refers to Walther Eichrodt's Theology of the Old Testament. At last I had found the gushing river of the uses and meaning and the interpretation of: A seret Had [Debar]im : TEN WORDS. **(END) 10**

These "Ten Words" are found in Exodus 20:1; 34: 1, 27f; Deuteronomy 4:10, 13, 36; 5:5,19; 9:10; and 10:2, 4. Exodus 34:28 is translated in K&D, "And He [Jehovah] wrote upon the tables the ten covenant words [a seret had[debar]im]." (END) 11 I found that most people are more interested in arranging the ten covenant words than they are in translating, explaining and / or living by them.

How could anybody ever teach/believe replacement theology?[1]

---

[1] Replacement Theology is the teaching that the church has replaced Israel in God's plan. More info is found: https://www.gotquestions.org/replacement-theology.html

I visited my Jewish Doctor, and he asked me what I had been doing? I told him that I had been studying Debar. He said, "BeBar Torah!" Yes, What a lovely believer!

> Hebrew: "DeBars" = The living Words of the Living God is found in Strong's Concordance number 1697.
>
> Greek: "Rema" = is used 70 times in the NT, and it's number 4487 in Strong's.

Eichrodt says: "the prophetic word achieves its effect not in opposition to the legal dabar but on the basis of it." (END) 12

DeBarim: { the plural of DeBar} and these words are all legal terms. These words are found in Deuteronomy 28, Leviticus 26 – described as DeBarim. But, in Deuteronomy 4:30; 30:1; and Joshua 21:45; 23:14 (Jeremiah 29:10; Hebrews 6:5 in the N.T. 1 Kings 8:36) they are referred to as "the good Word of Yahve."

Von Rad proclaims: "This 'theology of the word' was intended to give a systematic explanation of the phenomenon of the word of Yahweh, and this explanation, in its turn, was[is] to serve as a basis for the huge project of surveying the phenomenon of prophecy."

See again Von Rad (TMOP) which says, "It is the Deuteronomic History and it pictures Israel's History as a History of Yahweh's effective Word [Debar]," and because of this a 'Theology of the DeBar/Rema' must be written even though it is a huge project of surveying "the phenomenon of Biblical prophecy."

So, I am trying to write this chapter to show how huge this project really is, and this may be why it has been, as Von Rad rightly states, given only a "superficial glance by most OT scholars." (END) 13

An overview **MUST** be given to motivate Bible readers and scholars and to show them that the find in mining is well worth the digging. The DeBar not only 'has a profound meaning (Dr. Moody) in the Old Testament (OT), but it is *"profoundational"* [This word was used by my wife Betty] of all OT Spiritual Torahs /Theology, all OT Legislations Torahs, and all OT Civil Torahs. Eichrodt, sums it up: "And the foundation laid for all future legislation, below (under Heaven). The prophetic Word of God [**Debar**] achieves its effect not in opposition to the legal dabar, but on the basis of it." (END) 13. This confirms that the 'Divine Debar/ Will of YHWH' by which the people's way of life [was] is determined.   Hallelujah to YHWH!

This DeBar Word Speech/Act/ Event which reveals itself in Salvation History may be <u>static</u> as some say: "frozen in the OT," but it is also made <u>dynamic</u> in the OT by the Ruach ha-Kodesh, which is "the Holy Spirit as known in the New Testament (NT). The Word is made dynamic in the New Testament by the Holy Spirit.

[the accent is on the last syllable "Kodesh" = "desh" which makes this Hebrew word "the Holy Spirit" not the spirit of the holy one as in a saint if it was "Kodosh")

Eichrodt concluded by saying, "Furthermore, it was the 'association of <u>Spirit</u> and <u>Word</u>', [this is always the correct order, (1 Samuel 23: 3; Proverbs 1:23] as this in its various forms determined the O. T. conception of the Spirit, which was incomparably fulfilled in the N.T.

Belief in the Holy Spirit, through whose power Jesus accomplished his prophetic mission, and in the Paraclete [the Holy Spirit] sent by Him, who continually renews his [DeBars/Rema Words] work in the community, and gives to the members of the Body [soma of Messiah] a share in a life of [His] divine power." (END) 14

This association of the Ruach ha-kodesh and Debars/Remata together is the correct way that they must be received and translated and used in the Old and New Testaments. It says in Proverb 1:23 in the New American Standard Bible (NASB), "Turn to **My** reproof, Behold, **I** will pour out **My** Spirit on you; **I** will make **My** Words known to you." This again confirms the order: it is always Rauch ha-kodesh first; Then, the DeBars/Remata will be revealed with the Power to effect or to accomplish the result. This order is determined in the OT conception of the Ruach ha-kodesh and the Debars/Remata which is incomparably fulfilled in the NT by the Holy Spirit speaking the Rema as it says, *["Now the Ruach clearly says that in later times some will fall away from the faith, following deceitful spirits and teachings of demons."* I Timothy 4:1]. TLV

The Spirit speaks the word (retow) expressively. This Divine Power in our life is why the search is well worth the life and time of all Believers! The DeBars/Remata Speech/Act/Event by A/Y is "something said as something done" in our lives and in the History of Abram [Genesis 11:31ff; 12:1-3]/to Abraham [Genesis 17:5], Isaac, and Jacob. Hallelu-praise to YHWH!!

CHAPTER 2

I found an interesting phrase in Dr. Hort's, *Judaiatic Christianity:* "The DeBars in the Hexateuch: the first six books of the FIRST COVENANT. The first time the word DeBar appears in the FIRST COVENANT is in Genesis 15:1, 4, and the results of the DeBar is found in Genesis 15:6, where it says that "the Word [Debar] of A/Y appears to Abram in a vision." A/Y said to Abram, "Do not fear, Abram, I am a shield to you;" [This is what is read in the NASB concordance. In other translations one reads: 'Your very great Reward.'] When we know Him or are known by Him [Galatians. 4:9a *"But, now you have come to know God – or rather you have come to be known by God."*] we have a shield who protects us. Just to reiterate: When God has spoken the words in our heart, we will find that they are our shield and very great reward.   (END)   15

Does A/Y know that you and I are completely committed to Him? What a <u>very</u> great difference this makes in our life. And, what a <u>very</u> <u>great</u> <u>reward, or shield</u> A/Y is <u>in and to</u> us!

Paul the Apostle had to qualify that word in Galatians 4:9a, because, he/we in our finite mind can never know A/Y in His infinite thoughts, as Isaiah 55:8-9 declares. But we can have the Mind of Messiah as 1 Corinthians 2:16 says, [For "who has known the mind of ADONAI, that he will instruct Him?" But we have the mind of Messiah."], as explained in verses 6-15:

> We do speak wisdom, however, among those who are mature— but not a wisdom of this age or of the rulers of this age, who are coming to nothing. 7 Rather, we speak God's wisdom in a mystery—a wisdom that has been hidden, which God destined for our glory before the ages. 8 None of the rulers of this age understood it—for if they had, they would not have crucified the Lord of glory. 9 But as it is written,
>
> > "Things no eye has seen
> >   and no ear has heard,
> >   that have not entered the heart of mankind—
> > these things God has prepared
> >   for those who love Him."[b]
>
> 10 But God revealed these things to us through the Ruach.[c] For the Ruach searches all things—even the depths of God. 11 For who among men knows the things of a man, except the man's spirit within him? In the same way, no one knows the things of God except the Ruach Elohim. 12 Now we have received not the spirit of the world, but the Spirit who is from God—so we might come to know the things freely given to us by God. 13 These things we also speak—not in words taught by human wisdom but in words taught by the Ruach, explaining the spiritual to the spiritual.
>
> 14 Now a natural man does not accept the things of the Ruach Elohim, for they are foolishness to him; and he cannot understand them, because they are spiritually discerned. 15 But the one who is spiritual discerns all things, and he himself is discerned by no one. For:

16 "who has known the mind of Adonai,
that he will instruct Him?"[d]
But we have the mind of Messiah.

Genesis 15:4 says: [Then behold, the word of Adonai came to him saying, "This one will not be your heir, but in fact, one who will come from your own body will be your heir."] Read Paul's discussion In Romans 4.

As we see in Genesis 15:6, ["Then he believed in Adonai and He reckoned it to him as righteousness."], the DeBar always produces results, for when A/Y speaks the DeBar, there is always an event, an act, a result in history. This verse is the bedrock of all Judaic/Hebraic/Messianic Theology. It is the <u>most</u> important statement found in the FIRST COVENANT, and it is the basis of the entire NT. "Then he [Abram] believed in the Lord, and He reckoned it to him as righteousness." This thesis, this belief, this faith, controls all the Promises found in the FIRST COVENANT and all Promises fulfilled in the NT.

> *"For we also have had Good News proclaimed to us, just as they did. But the word they heard did not help them, because they were not unified with those who listened in faith." Hebrews 4:2 TLV*

Paul bears witness of this in Romans 1:5: *"Through Him we have received grace and the office of emissary, to bring about obedience of faith among all the nations on behalf of His name.*   TLV

Now, look at this version: "Through whom [Jesus Christ] [Jesus Christ Messiah our A/Y] we have received grace and apostleship to bring about the obedience of faith [Greek: "the hearing of faith"] among the Gentiles for His name's sake." [See: Romans 16: 25c- 26 in the sidebar]

A/Y speaks His DeBarim /Remata and we must **hear** and believe them. As Hebrews 4:2b says, "But the word they heard did not help them, because they were not unified with those who listened in faith." When these words are mixed with faith, they become a powerful life-changing force in our lives. Abram received this Word [DeBars] of A/ Y as a vision in the day time.

> *the mystery which has been kept secret for long ages* [26] *but now is revealed and through the Writings of the Prophets has been made known to all the nations, according to the commandment of the eternal God to bring about obedience of faith—*
>
> *Romans 16:25c – 26 TLV*

In our study of the Debar words in the OT, we will not be able to discuss all the Debars. We are going to just hit the "Mount Everest peaks" where snow stays all year, and the fire of A/Y's Shekinah Glory remains in the great Debars' revelations of that which has taken place in History.

Eichrodt says: "The effect of the Spirit was [is] to make the word [Debar] from the past live, and to bring it into contact with the present in a binding immediacy." (END) 16   The Holy Spirit fuses together the past DeBars/Rematas in the FIRST COVENANT and in the new NT, and they live in the present in great and binding powerful/immediacy! This is why they must be studied and known by all who are believers!

Jesus Christ confirms this 'powerful/immediacy' as He taught His Twelve Disciples as seen in John 14:26: "But the Helper, the Ruach ha-

Kodesh whom the Father will send in My name, will teach you everything and remind you of everything that I said to you." How foolish we are when we try to understand and do the Will of A/Y without the Holy Spirit's help, Whom the Father sends/gives in His [Jesus Christ's] Name.

Because we have a question in Genesis 18:10 that says: "Is anything [Word DeBar] too difficult [wonderful] for A/Y?" It is repeated to Mary, in Luke 1:37 in the NT: "For nothing [here <u>Debar</u> is **Rema** and translated as nothing] will be impossible with God." [TLV] This example shows just one way **Rema** is **translated** in the FIRST COVENANT or rather **mistranslated**.

This shows how the first Messianic believers believed the Debars/Remata Words of A/Y, and we must say what Mary said Luke 1:38, "Behold, the bondslave [Greek: "doulee" = female slave] of the Lord; may it be done to me according to your word [**Rema**]." May it be done to us/through us according to A/Y Debars/Remata Words.

We see in Moses how Adonai became A/Y in Exodus 3:14 and, before that He was El in all the Sematic World. A. B. Davidson points out, "but because of progressive revelation he became El Shaddai in the Patriarchal age, and to Moses He became Yah". (END) 17 It was to/through Moses that Adonai became Yah to Israel also. So, He must <u>now</u> be A/Y to us.

A/Y put His DeBars in Moses mouth. In Exodus 4:15 it says "You are to speak to him and put the words in his mouth. I will be with your mouth and with his, and teach you what to do." [TLV] This is what the Debarim /Remata does – they teach us what to **do** and to say.

Eichrodt says,

"*Side by side with the Spirit [Ruach ha Kodesh] which God causes to rest upon His people the Words[DeBarim] which He has put in their mouth* ___form___ *the* ___content___ *of the everlasting covenant [which He cut with His People] linking Israel with its God," [and in a foot-note, 'It was the Spirit which gave rise to the Word [DeBar] of God uttered in times past and now of normative significance in the present, and which is at the same time the power giving life to the community'].* " *(END) 18*

> 12 So then, the Torah is holy, and the commandment is holy and righteous and good. 13 Therefore did that which is good become death to me? May it never be! Rather it was sin working death in me—through that which is good—so that sin might be shown to be sin, and that through the commandment sin might become utterly sinful. 14 For we know that the Torah is spiritual; but I am of the flesh, sold to sin. Romans 7:12-14 [TLV]

This long quote is necessary to see the full impact, significance, scope, and important of the Spirit and the Words of A/Y being side by side in both the OT and NT.

Exodus 19:4b-6 introduces a new revelation unto the FIRST COVENANT. "And how I bore you on eagles' wings, and brought you unto Myself. Now, then if you will indeed Ob<u>ey My</u> voice and <u>keep My</u> covenant, then you shall be <u>My</u> possession [con. Special treasure] and shall be to <u>Me</u> a kingdom of priests and a Holy Nation." A/Y was/is not just looking for a nation, but He was/ is looking for a Kingdom of Holy Priests/Holy Nation of believers

In Exodus 20:1 Then Adonai spoke this Debars: "a seret had Debarim" unto Moses; ten words of Torah or Commandments. Also, Exodus 34:1: "Now the Lord said unto Moses 'Cut out for yourself two stones tablets like the first ones, and I will write on the tablets the words [a seret had DeBarim] that were on the former tablets which you shattered.' " How can anyone ever believe that these DeBars/Torah can pass away? Paul says in Roman 7:12, 14 "So then, the law [Torah] is holy, and the commandments [a seret had Debarim] is holy, and righteous and good', and v14 'For we know that the Law [Torah] is spiritual, but I am of flesh, sold unto sin   [concordance: the Greek says "having been sold under sin]". This shows how Paul understood the Torah/Commandments. So, how could anything so Holy and Spiritual ever end or be done away with as many theologians and some believers are saying today?

Von Rad, "The classic expression of this aspect of prophecy is in Amos' word--her very election made the threat to Israel all the greater [Amos 3:1ff]! This is therefore the first occasion in Israel when 'law' in the proper since of the term was preached." (END) 19   This is explained in 1 Peter 4: 18 which says, "If it is with difficultly that the righteous be saved, what [where will appear] will become of the godless man and the sinner?" Notice, Peter joined the godless person with the sinner. Remember, You can't just **believe** the Ten Words you must **keep/do** them, or you/we are a carnal believer. [1 Corinthians 3:1-4]

And so, it must be preached today as Paul does in the Epistles of Galatians and Romans. Anything less is another gospel Galatians 1:6-9: not the Gospel of the OT or NT. Deuteronomy 4:10b "Adonai said to me, 'Gather the people to Me and I will make them hear My Words [DeBarim], so that they learn to fear Me all the days that they live on the earth, and so that they teach their children.' " Adonai/Yah will and does make all Mankind hear the DeBarim, [as recorded] in Psalms. 19:2-3; Ro 1: 19; 10:18 which says "But I say, have they never heard? Indeed they have for 'Their voice has gone out into all the earth, and their words to the ends of the world.' "

It also says, in Deuteronomy 4:13: "And He declared to you His covenant, which He commanded you to **do The Ten Words** – and He wrote them in two tablets of stone." Without keeping the ten Words there is no lasting Covenant with Adonai' YHWH. The Jews tried by works of the Law to be righteous but were not able to be righteous. Because it says in Romans 8:3-4 TLV,

> *"For what was impossible for the Torah---since it was weakened on account*
> *of the flesh---God has done. Sending His own Son in the likeness of sinful*
> *flesh and as a sin offering, He condemned sin in the flesh—so that the*
> *requirement of the Torah might be fulfilled in us, who do not walk according*
> *to the Ruach."*

16

This is why we must keep walking in the Spirit as it says in Galatians 5:25 TLV, "If we live by the Ruach, let us also walk by the Ruach." Let us keep walking in the Ruach HaKodesh.

Deuteronomy 6:4-6 gives the Shema which is one of the greatest/ most repeated Words in Judaic /Hebraic Theology. And it is illustrated by the DeBars, written in your heart by the Spirit of the Living God [2 Corinthians 3:3]. The Words [DeBars] in v6, [These words, which I am commanding you today, are to be on your heart.] you must read/memorize it so that it can be written in your heart.

Deuteronomy 8:3d says "that He might make you understand [know] that man does not live by bread alone, but man lives by everything [DeBarim] that proceeds out of the mouth of Lord". Here, DeBarim is translated as "everything" and this was repeated by our Jesus Christ Messiah in Matthew 4:4 and Luke 4:4.

Deuteronomy 18:17-22 states how we are to know the real prophet from a presumptuous prophet which in verse 17-18 says "The Lord said to me, 'They have [con. Done well what they have spoken] spoken well, I [A/Y] will raise up a prophet from among their countryman [con, brothers] like you and I will put My Words in his mouth, and he shall speak to them all that I have command him.' " This is explained in Isaiah 51: 16 which says, "I [A/Y] have put My Words in your mouth and have covered you with the shadow of My Hand." This is the only covering that we ever need because as we go on **believing** [1 Thessalonians 1:13b declares it goes on **working** as our covering] we can have this Power/Shadow/Covering of A/Y Hand if we go on believing.

Deuteronomy 30:14 says: "But the word [DeBar] is very near you, in your mouth and in your heart, that you may observe it". This is another great verse found in the FIRST COVENANT and is repeated and expanded by Paul' in Romans 10:8. It proves what Paul says in Romans 1: 19-21, "For even though they knew God, they did not honor Him as God or give thanks, but they became futile in their speculations, and their foolish hearts were darkened." So, every person knows in his/her heart that there is a God. As verse 20d declares, "So that they/[we] are without excuse." Again, in 10:18 Paul makes full use of this verse when he said "What does it say? 'The Word [Rema] is near you, in your mouth and in your heart' – that is, the Word [Debar/Rema] of faith which we are preaching."

Some say that this is not what the FIRST COVENANT says. But, all one has to do is to see Psalm 19: 1-4 which confirms this great truth, and then connect Romans 10: 18 for Paul's discussion of Psalms 19: 4 which says: "But I say, surely they have never <u>heard</u>, have they? Indeed they [We] <u>have</u>: Their voice has gone out into all the earth, and their words [DeBar] to the ends of the earth." Most scholars will not discuss this verse as it <u>must</u> be discussed to understand Paul's Hebraic theology here, and in Romans 1:18-21, and 10:18.

> Thank You A/Y for afflicting Us and harassing us for our good!!
>
> Psalm 118: 18; 119:67

Dr. Dale Moody, does as he notes: "This question of hearing makes again the point that Israel has <u>heard</u>, but this time he goes beyond Israel to claim there is a universal gospel proclaimed in the whole order of creation Psalms 19:4." How could mankind be without excuse if they had not <u>heard</u> and <u>know</u> as both Psalms 19:4 and Romans 1:18-21;

10:18 which says/proclaims/ it loudly and clearly. **Indeed**, they/we have **Heard**, and Hebrews 9:27 says "And just as it is appointed for men to die once, and after that the judgement." (END) 20

K&D comments about the DeBar in the FIRST COVENANT. It is "When Deuteronomy [in 32:47] makes Moses exclaim 'this **Debar** is your <u>life.'</u>" It is true in both the OT and the NT, where Jesus Christ said in John 14:6 "I am the Way, Truth, and the <u>Life</u>, and no one, comes to the Father but through Me." (END) 21

<u>Joshua</u> sums up the teaching of the OLD TESTAMENT on the Debars/ Words and issues a warning to all the OT and NT believers.

Joshua says "Now behold, today I am going the way of all the earth [we all are], and you know in all your hearts and in all your souls that 'not <u>one</u> word of all the good Words [DeBarim] which the Lord spoke concerning you has failed; all have been fulfilled for you, not one of them have failed.'" This great statement was made as Joshua looked back over the history of the Jewish people, and as he looked back over his own life. We, who are believers, can look back over our own lives, and we can boldly say that not <u>one</u> good DeBar/Rema that A/Y has spoken to us has failed: Hallelujah what a Savior AND Lord!

Now, consider the way "DeBar" is translated sometimes *as a thing* rather than *as the DeBar.* In Genesis 41:28, 32, Moses writes: "This is the **thing** [Debar] which I have spoken to Pharaoh:

God has shown Pharaoh what He is about to do; and in 32b 'it means that the matter [DeBar] is determined by God.' " Moses spoke the thing in verse 28, but A/Y determined the matter [DeBar] in v 32. Dr. Dale Moody, in *The Broadman Bible Commentary comments on* verse 28: "This is my Message to Pharaoh" and in 32b ". . .the matter [DeBar] is divinely settled: God will presently bring it about.' " (END) 22 This is an example of how scholars have struggled with the translating of "the DeBar." Von Rad said in *The Message of Prophets*, that "92 percent relate to a prophetic oracle", and 92 percent of the time it should be translated as "DeBar," and I think he is correct. When this is done then we can see how basic the DeBar is in FIRST COVENANT Judaic/Hebraic Theology/Legislative/Civil life.   (END) 23

> *"Now today I am about to go the way of all the earth. You will know with all your heart and with all your soul that not one word of the good things which Aᴅᴏɴᴀɪ your God spoke concerning you has failed to happen. All of them have come to pass for you; not one word has failed. ¹⁵ Now it will be that just as all the good things which Aᴅᴏɴᴀɪ your God has spoken to you have come upon you, so all the evil things will Aᴅᴏɴᴀɪ bring upon you, until He has wiped you off this good land which Aᴅᴏɴᴀɪ your God has given you."*
>
> *Joshua 23:14-15 TLV*

Joshua 23:14-15 reiterates the **Promise** about the good DeBar, and the **Warning**. "It shall come about that just as all the good DeBars which the Lord has spoken to you have come upon you, so the Lord will bring upon you all the threats." We are so thrilled to receive all the good Words and Promises, but most people and scholars do not believe that the threats are going to be brought upon all Israel and all believers who are not being sanctified by the Holy Spirit. *["For both He who sanctifies and those being sanctified are all from one—so He is not ashamed to call them brothers and sisters. . .* Hebrews 2:11 TLV]

To illustrate this point, all one has to do is to look at Jeremiah 15:11, where the scholars will not translate the Hebrew according to K&D, who are conservative scholars, which says: "The question remains – whether we are to take "rrw" [2] according to the Hebrew's usage: I <u>afflict</u> thee to thy good, <u>harass</u> thee to thine advantage or the Aramaic 'I strengthen thee or support thee to thy good'; We prefer the latter rendering, because the saying: I afflict thee, is not true of God.' " (END) 24

Thank You A/Y for <u>afflicting</u> David/Us [Psalms 118: 18; 119:67], and <u>harassing</u> us for our good!!

How can anyone, who has read the FIRST COVENANT (OT) and the NEW COVENANT (NT), make such a statement as the above? The history of the FIRST COVENANT and NT refutes this statement, and most preachers who are preaching today only preach that A/Y is a loving God. This is another one of those "new gospels" spoken about above in Galatians 1:6-9. He is a loving God, but He is also a Holy [Kodesh] A/Y, and He does hold all people/all of us accountable for their/our sins and that sin always has a serious penalty. If He did not, He would have to apologize to our Messiah Jesus Christ because He laid all our iniquities on Him (Isaiah 53).

---

[2] [EDITOR: clarification: "rrw" is a Hebrew word without the vowels]

"The Prophets" do show how A/Y dealt with His Prophet. In Exodus 4:12, 15, 16:

> *"Now then go. And I, even I, will be with your mouth, and teach what you are to say." v15 "You are to speak to him [Aaron] and to put the words [Debarim] in his mouth, and I, even I, will be with your mouth and his mouth, and I will teach you what you are to do', v 16 "Moreover, he shall speak for you to the people; and he will be as a mouth for you, and you will be as a God [Elohim] to him."*

K & D comments, "The Targum softens down the word 'God' [elohim] into "master , and teacher.' " This is what "Elohim" means most times in the FIRST COVENANT, as John 10:34 says. (END) 25

Moses was the first prophet as Richard Foster declares: "So Moses became their mediator. Thus began the great ministry of the prophets whose function was to hear God's Word and bring it to the people." (END) 26   He certainly was an example and a pattern that all the Prophets should follow in speaking what DeBars words that A/Y put in their mouth. See 1 Peter 4:11a which says, *"Whoever speaks, let it be as one speaking the utterances* [the Living Logi "This is the one who was in the community in the wilderness, with the angel who spoke to him on Mount Sinai, and with our fathers. He received living words to pass on to us. - Acts 7:38 TLV] *of God."*

We will now turn to the Judges, Early Prophets and prophetic books in our next chapter.

CHAPTER 3

Now, we come to the books of the **Judges** and the **Prophets.** There is a very important statement in 1 Samuel 9:9 which explains Judges. It is: "(Formerly in Israel, when a man went to inquire of God, he said, "Come, let's go to the seer"—for today's prophet was formerly called a seer.)" This covers the Judges who were sought out for their wisdom and upon whom the Ruach dwells. And, so Judges is sort of a bridge between the Hexatude and Moses the first prophet and 1 Samuel the last judge and the beginning of the early Prophets.

The context must guide the translation!

In Judges 2:1 "The angel of the Adonai came. . ." Who is this Angel of A/Y that keeps appearing to the People of Adonai? Some say that it was the Messiah or the prince of the host of Israel. Joshua 5:13-14 explains who kept appearing in an intermittingly way, and OT people of Israel were looking/hoping for the permanent presence of a Messiah.

The best example of the difference between when DeBar should be translated as "thing" or "Word" is found Judges 6:29, which says:

" 'Who did this thing?' They said, 'Gideon, the son of Joash did this thing.' " It could not mean a word spoken, but a thing done because of the DeBar that was spoken to him. This shows how the context must guide the translation, or the word or thing will be a misinterpretation. We are not going to spend much time in Judges because we are hurrying along to get to the Prophets who have a clear understanding/interpretation of the DeBarim of Adonai/Yah.

The best summation of Judges is found in 1 Chronicles 17:6, which show why their call was given by A/Y.   " Wherever I went throughout all Israel, did I ever speak a word to any of the judges of Israel whom I commanded to shepherd My people, saying, 'Why have you not built Me a   house of cedar?' " What a beautiful picture of how A/Y walked with and shepherded all Israel, and how that He has made it possible for all OT and all NT believers to walk with Him. "If we live in the Spirit let us also walk [follow] in the Spirit [Galatians 5:25]."

The DeBar in the early Prophets, beginning with 1 Samuel 1:23 where Elkanah says, "Only the Lord establishes His Word [De -Bar] and fulfills it." K&D discusses, and says this is not what A/ Y says. "By 'His word' we are not to understand some direct revelations from God respecting the birth and destination of Samuel, as the Rabbis suppose." They say it was not a Divine revelation, but it was not some word from Eli. This shows that they did not understand what the DeBars from A/Y means. It is "Something said as well as something done." (END) 27

Dr. A.T. Robertson confirms that it should be translated as "A Hebraistic and vernacular use of 'rhema' [something said] as something done." This confirmation means that both DeBar and Rema should be translated as other Rabbis say, when speaking about what A/Y is speaking, and not as the Rabbis think about Eli's words, nor about words we speak. (END) 28

In 1 Samuel 3:1 TLV: "Now, the boy Samuel was in service of Adonai [**In the same light, see Acts 13:2 which says, "While they were serving the Lord and fasting, the Ruach ha-Kodesh [Holy Spirit] said 'Set apart for [to] me Barnabas and Saul for the work to which I have called them."]** under Eli. In those days the word of Adonai was rare—there were no visions breaking through." Holy Spirit teach us how we can minister to A/Y more effectively!

> **Our goal is that others SEE the living "WORD" in us and be saved, delivered, healed and receive the gift of the Holy Spirit!**

Maybe, this is why they/we are not hearing/seeing more DeBars/Remata Words revealed/fulfilled to us and through us [Galatians 3:5] today, since we are not spending enough time fasting /praying /ministering to our Wonderful Adonai/Yah/Jesus Christ. The Lord created us, as the only part of His creation in the Universe who could respond to and minister to Him. He desires us to worship Him in spirit and in truth. [John 4:23]

Acts 6:2b has it "It is not desirable for us to neglect the word **[logon]** of God in order to serve tables, Marshall shares the meaning of verse four in Greek when he says: "But we will keep to the prayer and to the service of the Word." (END) 29 Our prayer should be: " A/Y help us to keep to the prayers and to the <u>reading/proclaiming/teaching</u> of the Word [logon] [1 Timothy 4:13-14] in order that we will not neglect our charisma and Your DeBars/Remata can be revealed unto us and through us to others."

1 Samuel 3:7 says, "Now Samuel did not yet know the Lord, nor has the word [DeBar] of the Lord yet been revealed to him." What a profound insight into OT theology and psychology. This is the plan of salvation: in the Old and New Testaments! It is spelled out. It is not enough to know about A/Y, but one/we must <u>know</u> Him before the DeBar/Rema Word can be revealed <u>unto/through</u> us. This is confirmed in the Gospel of John 3:3 -5: [*Yeshua* answered him, "Amen, amen I tell you, unless one is born from above, he cannot see the kingdom of God." v4 "How can a man be born when he is old?" Nicodemus said to Him. "He cannot enter his mother's womb a second time and be born, can he?" v5 *Yeshua* answered, "Amen, amen I tell you, unless one is born of water and spirit, he cannot enter the kingdom of God. TLV] where verse five points out: One must be born a second time (possess salvation) to **enter** the Kingdom Also in the book Romans 10:8ff.

Before A/Y can raise up a prophet, He must raise up a godly woman. That is why the story of Hannah is so loved by all OT and NT believers. See Psalms 68:12, which says: " The Lord gives the word—a great company of women proclaims the good news."

"The Lord gave the [DeBar: the KJV says "word," but, then it says "company" instead of women] command; and the women who proclaim the good tidings are a great host." This highlights and illustrates how important the study and the translation of the DeBar/Rema are, if we are going to understand them and experience them in our own lives daily. And, our goal is that others SEE the living DeBar/Rema in us, be **saved**, **delivered**, **healed** and **receive** the gift of the Holy Spirit [Acts 19:1-7].

A warning and a challenge is given in 1 Samuel 8:19 "So Samuel spoke all the words [DeBars] of A/Y to the people." Every prophet/preacher must speak all the Debars/Rema Words that A/Y reveals unto him/her. He/She cannot choose which words they want to speak, but most tell all that A/Y has spoken to them [see Numbers 22:35c "you shall speak only the word which I tell { I A/Y speak to }] you."

A warning is shown again in Isaiah 30:10 [TLV], which says, "They say to the seers, 'Do not see' and to the prophets, 'Do not prophesy to us what is right. Speak to us smooth words. Prophesy illusions."   It is also confirmed in Jeremiah 23:16 [TLV], "Thus says Adonai-Tzva'ot (host): 'Do not listen to the words of the prophets who are prophesying to you. They are leading you into illusion, speaking a vision of their own heart and not out of the mouth of Adonai."

Again, Jeremiah 23:32 [TLV] states, "Behold, I am against those who prophesy lying dreams" (Jeremiah 29:8c,

proclaims: "pay no attention to the dreams which you make them keep dreaming") declares Adonai, "and tell them and so lead My people astray with their lies and with their reckless boasts. Yet I never sent them or commanded them. Nor do they benefit this people at all. It is a declaration of Adonai."

Back to Isaiah 30:11 [TLV] which states, "Get out of the way! Turn away from the path! Let's hear no more about the Holy One of Israel."

The reason that Isaiah and Jeremiah is quoted here is because, we are being told today that we are to stop holding up and preaching about this Holy One of Israel. We are hearing this today in 2017: in the media, on television/radio and in print. Let us boldly hold up Holy A/Y.

David said in Psalms 119:11 TLV, " I have treasured your word in my heart, so I might not sin against You." Not only did he not sin against A/Y after, but he had fellowship with A/Y because He watches over His Word [DeBar to perform it. [Jeremiah 1:12-b] What a wonderful promise this is to all prophets/believers! And, all of His promises are "YES" in Christ, as 2 Corinthians 1:20 says so beautifully.

We need to look at a very important element here in 1 Samuel about prayer. Hannah's prayer in I:12ff, is well known by all OT/NT believers. It is an example to us for all prayers. Von Rad says: "That at least one of the main functions of the prophet was intercession." He refers to 1 Samuel 12:23 which says: "Moreover, as for me, far be it from me that I should sin against *ADONAI* by ceasing to pray for you! Yet I will keep instructing you in the good and straight way."

O, how we need instruction in prayers [see Luke 11:1], and the Holy Spirit <u>does</u>/<u>must</u> instruct us as it says in Romans 8: 26: **"In the same way, the *Ruach* helps in our weakness. For we do not know how to pray as we should, but the *Ruach* Himself intercedes for us with groans too deep for words."** And, as 1 John 2:27 shows clearly. (END) 30

Isaiah 59:15b-16 says, "Now the Lord saw, and it was displeasing in His sight that there was no justice. v16 And He saw that there was no man, and was astonished that there was no one to intercede." I wonder if A/Y is not astonished <u>now</u> that there are so few men and women today who are interceding for all the injustices in His world. This brings up a question about how prayer effects A/Y - "Does He change His essence or attributes when we pray?" Dr. A. B. Davidson states the difference between A/Y's <u>essence</u> and <u>attributes</u>. His <u>essence</u> is His Holiness, Love, Light, Life, and Sovereignty, which <u>cannot and </u>will <u>not</u> ever change. (END) 31

James I:17b confirms this: "Coming down from the Father of lights, with whom there is no variation or shifting shadow." Thanks to A/Y that in His essence there are no variation or shifting. <u>But,</u> His <u>attributes</u> do change which are: His Throne of Grace [I love that His Throne is called

Hesed/Grace: come boldly before His throne of Grace [repent] to <u>find</u> Mercy and <u>receive</u> Grace in time of need [G. boetheia: running and crying to A/Y to fine help in time of our need Hebrews 4:14] His Mercy, Longsuffering, Chastening, and Wrath can/do change when we pray/confess our sins, and we asks/receives forgiveness of all of our sins [stop sinning] as Exodus. 20:20 and 1 John 1: 9 says. Praise The Lord!

The Augsburg Confession says that "the Protestant perfection is the perfection of repentance and the fear [and I would add: the perfection of 'Holiness in the fear of the Lord' 2 Corinthians 7:1] of the Lord," of Adonai/Yah. (END) 32

This brings up an important idea that is very clear in Exodus 15: 11b: *"Who is like You among the gods, O Lord? Who is like You, Majestic* [Glorified: K&D translates it "Glorified as a verb and not a noun because A/Y is Glorified when we allow his Holiness to be manifested <u>in</u>/<u>through</u> us. . ." See Romans 8:30f (END) 33] *in Holiness, Awesome in praises, and Working wonders?"* Only Adonai /Yah can/does work signs/wonders/miracles in/through us.

We need to look a 1 Samuel 16: 13b-14 because it holds the key to a very important translation, interpretation, and understanding of the names of Adonai/Yah /versus [gods Exodus.15:11b] Elohim, where verse 13b says, "The Spirit of the A/Y came nightly upon David from that day forward [upward] and verse 14 says: "Now, the Spirit of the A/Y departed from Saul, and an evil spirit from the Lord [elohim] terrorized him". This statement has led many scholars to say that true Hebraism was monotheistic and not a trinity. But the correct interpretation of the Hebrew says something quite differently.

K&D, argues, "But a higher evil power which took possession of him stirred up the feelings, ideas, imagination, and thought of his soul. This demon is called 'an evil spirit [con. coming] from Elohim, because he had sent it as a punishment, and as 'a spirit of [Elohim]' as being a supernatural, spiritual, evil power, but never 'The Spirit of Jehovah' because His Spirit is proceeding from the Holy God.' " (END) 34   This quote shows that the Spirit of Yahweh can never be the evil spirit of Elohim, because the Holy Spirit generates and fosters the Spiritual/Divine Life.

A. B. Davidson says, "This expression is no doubt, wrongly translated in our Version as 'son of God'. The name Elohim is used both for God and angels.' " (END) 35   It is good to find someone else who confirms what the translation and interpretation says which also agrees with K&D said above.

Two further statements by A.B. Davidson may help clarify this. On page68 it says, "In the times before Abraham, the name of God was Elohim, or El; in the Patriarchal age it was El Shaddai from Abraham onwards; in the Mosaic age and henceforward it was Yahweh." The next one is on p. 41 "The Name El is the oldest name for God: Babylonain ilu, where u is nominate case; Arabic: ilah; Aram: elah." This book is credited with being the first book ever written about 'Biblical Theology' by A. B. Davidson, in 1904 . (END) 36.

WOW! What a clarification of the terms A/Y and Elohim. Elohim is frequently ambiguous in the OT, as the NT proves in John 10: 34, when Jesus Christ referred to men being called Elohim, as it is also confirmed in Psalms 82: 6; and 97:7. This is an amazing discovery for OT and NT theology. Psalms 50:1 has all the terms correctly: El/Elohim/Yah:

El, the Semitic gods,

El Shaddai: A sematic word for the Almighty which everybody sees in the creation (Exodus 6:3)

Elohim: Is to be feared.

Adonai/YHWH: The covenant **making/keeping/loving** [hesed] of A/Y which shows a progressive revelation and understanding of these terms in Judaic/Hebraic/Messianic OT Theology.

The difference is shown by Walter Eichroth, (epi. cit in vol. 1 p.191) which says "Adonai/-YHWH shares that 'opposition to all that is merely naturalistic' 'and part of the phenomenal world, which is characteristic of the worship of El." (END) 37

This is <u>proven</u> in Deuteronomy 4:31, "Because He [Adonai/Yah[loved your fathers, and therefore He chose their descendants[his seed con.] after them. And He personally [with His presence con.' by His Face K&D'] brought you from Egypt by His great power."

And in Hosea 13:4a "I have been the Lord [YHWH] your God since Egypt." This shows the progressive revelation also as it is shown in 1 Peter 3:15: "But sanctify Christ [Messiah] in your hearts as Lord", for many people know Him as Savior [and are fleshly believers 1 Corinthians 3:1-4] but do not know Him as Lord by sanctifying Him in their heart.

This also confirmed in Psalm 119, where the Word "Yah" is used 22 times together with the DeBar which is used 42 times. K&D comments "God's hand, ver. 173, and God's Word [DeBar] afford him succour; the

two are involved in one another, the Word is the medium of His Hand".
(END) 38

Ezekiel 1:3 says: "The Word came expressively", and "there the Hand of the Lord came upon him." The hand represents the Power of A/Y being present to save, to deliver, and to heal when allowed. HalleluYah!

In summary regarding 1 Samuel's use of "the Word," a statement is found in 3:19 which says, "Thus Samuel grew up and the Lord was with him and let none of his Debars fall to the ground." What a legacy!

2 Samuel shows a clear picture of the role of the Prophet, and his messages.

In 7:2 we are introduced to Nathan the Prophet, to distinguish from Nathan, David's son. Nathan is listening to David talk about how he wanted to build a house for A/Y. So, Nathan said A/Y is with you "go do what is in your mind", but most of the time what is in our mind is not what A/Y wants. [Acts 16:6ff] Verse 4 -13 continues:

> *"But in the same night the DeBar of A/Y came to Nathan, saying, "Go and say to David, Thus says the Lord, 'are you the one who should build Me a house to dwell in?" "The Lord also declares to you that the Lord will make a house for you; I will raise up your descendent [seed] after you, and He shall build My House."*

A prophetic DeBar/Promise was delivered to David that became the sure mercies of David [Isaiah 55: 3d]. That is a prophet oracle about the Messiah. This was/is a very powerful/positive message even until today, but Nathan delivers another negative message in 12ff.

A parable about "sheep" was given to David by Nathan, [2 Samuel 12:1-4] and v5 "Then David's anger burned against the man, and he said to Nathan 'As the Lord lives, surely the man who has done this [con is a son of death] deserves death.' " v 7 "Nathan then said to David 'You are the man,' " and v9 asks, "Why have you despised the Word [DeBar] of the Lord by doing this evil in His sight?" Every time we believers do evil in A/Y sight we are despising His Debars/Rema because they are in our mouth and hearts. This is why we <u>must</u> be instructed about His 'a seret had Debarim' in both the OT and NT.

To sum up 2 Samuel, we need to look at chapters 22-23 which are two poems, and are some of the oldest written in Hebrew in the OT. We will look at 22:31, which says, "As for God, His way is blameless [con complete]: The Word [DeBars] of the Lord is tested; He is a shield [and reward] to all who take refuge in Him." When we reject His Debars we cannot claim Him as our shield or take refuge in Him because "He is a shield only those who obey His DeBars." When we have rejected His DeBars He will reject us and not be our shield and refuge.

> *When we reject His Debars [Words] we cannot claim Him as our shield or take refuge in Him!*

The last part that we will look at is 23:1-2. These verses declare: "Now these are the last words [DeBars] of David. David, the son of Jesse declares, the man who was raised on high declares, the anointed of the God of Jacob, and the sweet psalmist of Israel, v2 the Spirit of the A/Y spoke by me, and His Word [a poetic word for DeBar] was on my tongue." What a testimony of David is given in these verses! They refute the argument that the Ruach ha KoDesh is not a part of early Judaism for they were written by 1000 BC. This argument has caused so much misunderstanding about the Ruach in the OT, and also even in the NT. People who were looking for an excuse to reject the truth about the Ruach ha-KoDesh found it in many of OT writers. The NT changes all this into a positive revelation by the coming of the Holy Spirit and fulfillment of His Power.

1 Kings is a transition between David and Solomon. 1 Kings 2:1-4 gives insight into this moment in the history of Israel: "As David's time to die drew near, He charged Solomon, 'So that the Lord may carry out His promise [DeBars] which He spoke concerning Me, saying. . .' " The condition is that all Words [DeBars] are to be obeyed then/now if not the Word will not be fulfilled. See also Romans 9:6 which shows the Word has not failed.

1 Kings 6:11f "Now the word [DeBar] of the Lord came to Solomon saying, 'Concerning this house which you are building, if you will walk in My statutes, execute My ordinances, and keep all My commandment by walking in them, then I will carry out My word [DeBar] with you which I spoke to David your father.' " This should erase all beliefs, then and now, if there are any divine rights in OT or NT when one is not walking obediently before A/Y. See Acts 5:32.

In 1 Kings 17:1-2 Elijah is introduced as the Tishbite, who said to Ahab "As the Lord, the God of Israel lives, before whom I stand, surely there shall be no rain these three years, except by my word [DeBar]." "Then the word [DeBar] of the Lord came to him saying, "Go away." 1 Kings 17:3

K&D comments, "This abrupt appearance of Elijah cannot be satisfactorily explained." It 'indicates that in him the divine power of the Spirit appeared as *He* [italics and pronoun changed by author] was personified, and his life and acts were the direct effluence of the higher power by which he was impelled." (END) 39

We must also be impelled [carried along by the Spirit, 2 Peter 1:21], if we are going to speak for A/Y] by the Ruach Hakodesh and if we are going to be a slave/servant to Jesus Christ, Our Messiah/A/Y.

The widow whose son was raised by Elijah proclaimed (1 Kings 17:24 "Now I know that you are a man of God and that the word [Debar] of the Lord [A/Y] in your mouth is truth." O, that people could know that all Words of A/Y in our mouth are truth.

1 Kings 18:1 declares "Now it happened after many days that the word [DeBar] of the Lord came to Elijah in the third year," and the battle begins between Elijah and Jezebel's prophets. Read all these chapters and it will strengthen your faith.

Elijah proclaims, "O Lord, the God of Abraham, Isaac, and Israel, today let it be known that You are God in Israel and that I am your servant and I have done all these things at your word]Debar]. [1 Kings 18:36]

Von Rad asks, to whom or to what was Elijah going to speak? "What is, however, more likely is that he expected Yahweh to commission him to command the rain." (END) 40 When A /Y gives the DeBar that it is not going to rain, then He is able to give the DeBar for rain. As Genesis 18:14 and Luke 1:37 confirms this.

One last word about these prophets must be said. How do you know when a prophet's words are true or not? 1 Kings 22:21-22 says, "Then a spirit came forward and stood before the Lord and said, 'I will entice him' and the Lord said to him, 'How?' And he said 'I will go out and be a lying spirit [sheqer ruach] in the mouth of all his prophets.' " We <u>must</u> listen to what Paul wrote in I Thessalonians 5:16-22. HalleluYAh!

2 Kings 6:12 says: "One of his servants said, 'No my lord [elohim] O king; but Elisha, the prophet who is in Israel, tells the king of Israel the words [DeBars] that you speak in your bedroom.' "

So, we must be careful to speak the same love language to A/Y that we say in our bedroom to one another because A/ Y is listening. He wants to hear it also.

2 Kings 22:11 says:

> "When the king [Josiah] heard the words [Debar] of the book of the Law, he tore his clothes," and, 2 Kings 23:2d -3 adds: "And he [Josiah] read in their hearing the book all the words [DeBars] of the book of the covenant which was found in the house of the Lord, The king stood by the pillar and made a covenant before the Lord, to walk after the Lord, and to keep His commandments and His testimonies and statutes with all his heart and all his soul, to carry out the words [DeBars] of this covenant that were written this book. And all the people entered [took a stand in] the covenant."

We <u>**must**</u> read the Book also and <u>**take**</u> a stand on all OT/DeBarim; NTC/Remata.

CHAPTER 4

I was following the Kings James Version order of the books of the Prophets, and I was checked by the Holy Spirit. I was told that I had been overlooking an important part and long period of Israel's history. So, now we will look at the books of Amos and Hosea before Isaiah.

Since, we are following the Jewish Bible outline we will now turn to the Prophets. We are going to follow the historical and chronological outline given in K&D in which was worked out by F. Delitzsch who was a Messianic believer and both were antiquity Scholars. (END) 41

ALL THE DATES BELOW WERE GIVEN BY Dr. Delitzsch in their commentary work. These dates of the books are in their historical and chronological order:

Obadiah in Joram reign	889-884
Joel in Joash reigns	875-848
Jonah in Jeroboam II	r. 824-783
Amos in Jeroboam II	r. 810-783
Hosea in Jeroboam II	r 790-725
Micah in Jotham, A&H	758-710
Nahum in Hezekiah	r. 710-699
Habakkuk in Josiah	r. 650-628
Zephaniah in Josiah	r. 628-623
Haggai in Darius Hystaspea	519
Zechariah " "	519
Malachi in Artaxerxes L	433-424

This outline is given so that as one studies the Prophets he/she can see a relationship between the Prophets and the History of Israel.

SUGGESTED OUTLINE

The Old Testament

I. The Pentatude and the Hexatude
   A. Genesis
   B. Joshua

II. Judges – The Bridge between the Pentatude and the Hexatude and the Early Prophets
   A. Judges
   B. 1 Samuel
   C. 2 Samuel
   D. 1 Kings

III. The Classical Prophets
   A. Joel   889 – 884
   B. Jonah   824 – 783
   C. Amos   810—783
   D. Hosea   790—725
   E. Isaiah   750—710
   F. Micah   758—710
   G. Jeremiah
   H. Lamentations
   I. Ezekiel
   J. Habakkuk
   K. Haggai
   L. Zachariah
   M. Malachi

IV. The Writings

    A. Psalms

    B. Proverbs

    C. Job

    D. Song of Solomon

    E. Ruth

    F. Ecclesiastes

    G. Esther

    H. Daniel

    I. Ezra

    J. Nehemiah

    K. 1 & 2 Chronicles

The New Testament

I. The New Covenant

    A.   Matthew

    B.   Mark

    C.   Luke

II. Acts

III. The General Letters

    A. James/Jacob

    B. 1 Peter

    C. 2 Peter

    D. Jude

IV. The Pauline Epistles

    A. 1 Corinthians

    B. 2 Corinthians/Romans

V. John and Hebrews

    A. John

    B. Hebrews

VI. Revelation

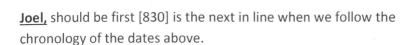

Joel, should be first [830] is the next in line when we follow the chronology of the dates above.

1:1 says "The Word of Lord that came to Joel, the son of Pethuel." This is the way the DeBars are delivered to many of the Prophets, and with the call and the deliverance comes the commission to <u>claim</u> and to <u>proclaim it</u>. Thanks be to A/Y.

2:11 says "The Lord utters His <u>Voice</u> before the Army; Surely His camp is very great, for strong is he who carries out His Word [DeBar]. The day of the Lord is indeed great and very awesome, and who can endure it." A/Y who carries out/pre-forms [Jeremiah 29:10 TLV] the Debar is strong and with this revelation come the strength of A/Y.

Another sidebar is found in the Hebrew Bible that starts at 2:28 which is 3:1 in H, and it is "It will come about after this that I will pour out My Spirit [Ruach] on all mankind [flesh]." Numbers 11: 17f, and all these verses refute all the argument about the Ruach not being a part of early Judaism, and it is a promise that was/is given by Jesus Christ again in Acts 1:8, and it was fulfilled to all believers in 2:1f, and to all [39] who are called later/will receive Him by faith.

Another sidebar is found in Jonah [825 which should be before Isaiah following Joel] is one of the greatest Missionary Books in all the Bible, and it shows what Adonai/Yah told Abraham in Genesis 17:5, when He changed His name from Abram, "exulted Father" to Abraham which means "Father of many nations."

 Jonah was called to go to Nineveh, and he went the other way. This sound like what most of us do when we are called.

Jonah was mentioned in 2 Kings 14:25 which help date the Book. A statement was made by Von Rad: "Of course, even in the earlier narratives about prophets, the 'hero' of the story was never the prophets himself, but rather Yahweh, who was glorified by the prophet." This is what all prophets must do: Their words are to Glorify A/Y, and not himself/herself. (END) 42

1:17-2:10 is one of the most "belittled" passages in all the Bible, because the LXX/KJV (known as THE SEVENTY) says a whale swallowed Jonah. But, it is confirmed by K&D that it was a "large shark or sea dog seen." I would have given a thousand dollars for this information while I was still in Seminary, for some of my so called liberal brothers. (END) 43

One of the great statements is all the OT is made in 4:1f: "But it greatly displeased Jonah and he became angry. He prayed to the Lord and said, 'Please Lord was not this what I said while I was still in my country? Therefore in order to forestall this I fled to Tarshish, for I knew that you are a gracious and compassionate God [what a great and Awesome Holy A/Y], slow to anger and abundant in lovingkindness, and one who relents concerning calamity.' " A/Y did not need Jonah's help, and He does not need ours either. He should have been jumping up and down and rejoicing because A/Y was/is so gracious and compassionate to Israel and to all Gentiles and to us. Was this not like what A/Y did and said to Peter in Acts 10?

There is a theory held by Universalists that injects words into a statement or concept, that changes the meaning to match their own philosophy. One such example is the theory of opposition that forced all of the Jewish men to divorce their non-Jewish wives.

Von Rad says again: "We have no knowledge of any 'universalists' opposition to the 'particularist' measures taken by Ezra and Nehemiah, and the book (Jonah) itself contains no evidence to support such a theory." (END) 44   But, this passage in Jonah does and so does Genesis 17:5; Isaiah 19; Psalms 19:4, and it is quoted above and discussed and repeated in Romans 4:18.

Amos was prophesying during the reign of Uzziah which was 783-742, according to John Bright. (END) 37   Amos 1:1 gives a wealth of information about Amos which is affirmed in 7:14 - "I am not a prophet, nor am I the son of a prophet; for I am a herdsman and a grower of the sycamore figs," and this is all we know about him. Amos 1:2 declares "Adonai/Yah roars from Zion, and from Jerusalem He utters His Voice."

This is parallel with what is said later by both Isaiah, in 2:15, and Micah in 4:13, and most likely it was repeated and based on what Joel 3:16 and Amos 1:1 said.

Most scholars are more concerning about who the author of Isaiah 2:15 and Micah 4:13 was and where they got the statement than that it was part of the prophetic Word of Adonai/Yah. However, it is strange that both copy it in their books.

Again, if we believe that the Ruach Ha kodesh is the author [L.auctor primaries] of the OT/ NT then we do not spend all our time trying find who the author is for "it stands written," according to Matthew 4:4a, by the Holy Spirit as Author.

Amos declares:

> 3:1 "Here this word [De Bar] which the Lord has spoken against you, sons of Israel, against the entire family [nation] which He brought up out of Egypt,
>
> v 2 "You only have I chosen [known: most think of the elect] among all the families of the earth; therefore, I will visit punish [visit on] you for all your iniquities,
>
> v3 "Do two men walk together unless they have made an appointment [agreement]?"

This refers to both the house of Israel/Judea, to the prophet, and it shows that all our iniquities will be punished. Therefore, we should try to keep all His Torahs/Debars/ Rema Words and try not to commit iniquities. Adonai/Yah takes all sins seriously. So, sins should become exceedingly and utterly sinful to us as to Paul in Romans 7:13.

He continues with one of the most profound insights in the OT, and it must be repeated:

> 4:1 *"Here this Word [DeBar], you cows of Basham you who are on the mountain of Samaria, who oppress the poor, who crush the needy, who say to your husbands, 'Bring more that we may drink i.e. 2:8; 6:6'. A/Y has sworn by His Holiness, Behold, the days are coming upon you when they will take you away with meat hooks, and you will go out through the breaches in the walls, each one straight before her, and you will be cast to Harman declares the Lord."*

This was written to correct the evil conduct in Israel which was started by Ahab/Jezebel [1 Kings 16:31-33] the most wicked rulers of all Israel. They were threatening true Judaism with this according to John Bright: "And that this was balanced by a cultic dualism: Yahweh God of Israel, or Baal Melqart god [god of darkness] of Samaria." (END) 45   This was about a century before Amos prophesied which confirms his concern and message. Anyone who oppress the poor and who crush the needy will have to answer to the Holy Adonai/Yah.

Amos gives us one of the most important statements in all the <u>annals</u> of History. "But let justice roll down like waters, and righteousness like an ever flowing stream." [5:24]

Dr. Richard J. Foster says that ". . . the worldwide revelation of this message is an actual historical event:

In Israel in the pre-exilic prophets 750-586 b.c Amos being the first

In India with the Upanishads [800-600]

In Gautama, the Buddha [560-480]

In Mahavira [599-527]

In China with Confucius [551-479]

In Lao Tza [604-517] and,

In Persia with Zarathushtra [660-583]

all in B.C." [indentions and column by author] (END) 46

The reason that I copied all these is that most of you might not have access to this book. It shows what one DeBar/Rema event/act/spoke Word from A/Y does. We must know/do all of them if we are going to be His follower and see His Miracles done, and do it <u>now</u>.

It is amazing how important these DeBar/Rema Words of Adonia/Yah are and how many religious leaders will reject them. In Amos 7:10f we have an example of Amariah confronting Amos. He reported him to Jeroboram the King of Israel. He said "The land is unable to endure all His Words [DeBars]."

This brought about 8:11-12

> " 'Behold, days are coming,' declares the Lord God, 'when I will send a famine in the land, not a famine for bread or a thirst for water, but rather for hearing the Word 's [DeBar] of the Lord. People will <u>stagger</u> from sea to sea and from the north to the east; they will go to and fro to seek the Word of the Lord, But they will not find it.' "

America has been staggering since 1932. We Americans were warned about this in 1932, by a young German prophet Dietrich Bonhoeffer who could not find the Word [Rema] being preached in any white Churches in New York City. He warned: "The theological atmosphere of the Union Theological Seminary is accelerating the process of the secularization of Christianity in America." (END) 47

This secularization of Christianity was completed in the 1950's by the preachers who were preaching the prosperity message and by 2013 most of our Churches had become cultural Churches which reflected the culture rather than the Messiah.

Bonhoeffer asks: "So, what stands in place of the Christian Message? It is an ethical and social idealism, borne by faith in progress that—who knows how—claims the right to call itself – 'Christian?' " Further, He says "There's no sense to expect the fruits where the Word is really no longer being preached" and, adds this, that he finally heard the gospel preached and saw its power manifested. The preacher at Abyssinian was a powerful figure named Dr. Adam Clayton Powell, Sr." (END) 48

This confirms what A/Y spoke to me in 1985, that the only hope for the secularized American Church was two-fold: Americans of African descent, and since 2002 the Messianic Movement made up of Jewish/Gentile Believers.

Von Rad said, "Hosea is the only 'writing prophet' of the Northern Kingdom." So now, we turn to **Hosea** to see what caused Israel leaders to reject the DeBar of Adonia/Yah. (END) 49

"The Word of the Lord which came to Hosea the son of Beeri." (1:1) [and the King James Version got this right: "The beginning of the Word of the Lord by Hosea." But, it should say 'When the Lord first spoke His Word [DeBar] through Hosea." (1:2)] This shows what I have believed since 1992, that Adonai/Yah <u>must</u> speak these DeBars/Remata to/through us before they have His miracle working power manifested in the "words."

It is true today, as Marshall says in the Greek: in 1 Timothy 4:1: "Now the Spirit says in Words [Retows] expressively," and as Adonia/Yah spoke through Hosea now the Holy Spirit <u>must</u> speak these Words [Remata] <u>in</u> /<u>through</u> us before they can become Signs/ Wonders/Miracles for and to others. (END) 50

In Hosea 4:1-2 the prophet repeats,

> *"Listen to the Word of the Lord, O sons of Israel, [O sons of America] for the Lord has a case against the inhabitants of the land [He has a case against America], because there is no faithfulness [truth] or kindness [Hesed] or knowledge of God in the land. (v2 There is swearing, deception, murder and adultery. They employ violence, so bloodshed follows bloodshed [1:4b I will visit the bloodshed of Jezreel upon the house of Jehu con.], v3a Therefore the land mourns, v5a My people are destroyed for a lack of knowledge!!"*

Many generations have made all kinds of advances in sciences and in Technology, but few have little knowledge of the Words of Adonai/Yah. And, because of this, the land of promise is mourning because we do not know the Lord. Hosea helps by what he records in 5:4b: "For a spirit of harlotry is within them, and they do not know the Lord [Refer back to 1:2c for the land commits flagrant harlotry from not following after the Lord concordance]." Thus, America, [as early Israel/maybe modern

Israel], has whored itself out from under Adonai/Yah hand/
covering/covenant/promises.

Hosea 6:4-5 gives Adonai's questions and judgments:

> *"What shall I do with you O Ephraim? What shall I do with you O
> Judah? For your loyalty [con. lovingkindness.] is like morning
> cloud, and like the dew which goes away early,(v 5) Therefore I
> have hewn them in pieces by the prophets, and I have slain them
> by the Words [DeBars] of My Mouth, and the judgments on you
> are like the light that goes forth,(v6) For I delight in loyalty
> [lovingkindness] rather than sacrifice, and the knowledge of God
> rather than burnt offerings."*

Verse five (5) has an awesome warning for the Prophets, because it
says, "Therefore, I have hewn them in pieces by the prophets, and I
have slain them by the Words [DeBars] of My mouth, and the
Judgments on you is like a light that goes forth."

 So, the prophet is not going to be accepted, but hated by the carnal
believers and the unbelieving world because no one likes to get hewn
and slain by His DeBars/Remata Words. This is what verse 6 above says
which is what I Samuel 15:22 spoke about 400 years before. Knowledge
of A/Y is required and not church attendance and sacrifices.

Hosea does not leave them, nor us, in the dark because he agrees with
Deuteronomy 10:12 (See 12:5) about what the Lord God requires of us:
"Therefore, return to your God, observe kindness [lovingkindness] and
justice, and wait for your God continually."

In Hosea 12:9a we have a statement that confirms our early argument
about the name of Yah was brought to the Israelites in Egypt by Moses

[s. Ex 6: 24]. It is "But I [Yah] have been the Lord your God since the land of Egypt." The whole Semitic World believes in El and Elohim, but only Israel became believers in Adonai/Yah, a covenant making and keeping A/Y when they saw all His signs, wonder, and miracle.

Hosea's greatest revelation is found in 13:12ff:

> "The iniquity of Ephraim [America] is bound up: his sin is stored up. The pains of childbirth come up him; he is not a _wise_ _son_, for [lit. it is the time that he should not tarry at the breaking forth of children]. Shall I ransom them from the power of Sheol? Shall I redeem them from death? O Death, where are your thorns? O Sheol where is your sting? Compassion will be hidden from My sight."

There will be no compassion for all those who will not be born from above [John 3:3,5]: they are not wise sons/daughters. There will be no compassion because they knew Adonai /Yah, see Romans 1:20; 10:18, and they will/have not receive (d) Him.

Of course, Paul developed this message completely in 1 Corinthians 15:50-58 after the resurrection of Messiah. Read/know all 1 Corinthians 15; it is truly Historical.

CHAPTER 5

Isaiah is the third book in the classic Prophets. K&D confirms the relationship between two verbs that run on the same rail in writing: "Isaiah commences in the same way, [ch. 1.2a], simple transposing the two parallel verbs '<u>hear</u>' and '<u>give</u> <u>ear.</u>' " (END) 51   Isaiah repeats the idea in verse 10, "Hear the Word [DeBar] of Yah, you rulers of Sodom, Give ear to the instruction [A seret hadDeBarim] the ten words of our A/Y, You people of Gomorrah." What a stinging rebuke of Israel/Judah and the carnal believers/unbelievers is given here by the prophet Isaiah.

Later, he spells out what this all means: "For the law [Torah] will go forth from Zion, and the Word [DeBar] of the Lord from Jerusalem." (Isaiah 2:3d) He is laying the foundation for his whole book and chapter 6. In 4:4 Isaiah teaches a <u>truth</u> that needs to be heard today. It is: "When the Lord has washed away the filth of the daughters [sons] of Zion and purged the bloodshed of Jerusalem from her midst, by the Spirit of <u>judgment</u> and the Spirit of <u>burning.</u>" This shows who the Holy Spirit is and what He does; not what is being preached and taught by many today.

K&D says: "The filth of the daughters [Sons] of Zion is the moral pollution hidden under their vain and coquettish finery; and the murderous deeds of Jerusalem are the acts of judicial murder committed by its rulers upon the poor and innocent." (END) 52
All are shut up in disobedience as Romans 11:32 says: "For God has shut up all in disobedience so [In order that] that He may show mercy to all."

When a person begins "believing God's Word, and the Holy Spirit is received, He, the Holy Spirit begins to judge: "For the Word of God is living and active and sharper than any two-edged sword and piercing as far as the division of soul/spirit, of both joints/marrow, and able to judge the thought/intentions of the heart [Hebrews 4:12]."

He searches all things: "For to us God revealed them through the Spirit; for the Spirit searches all things even the depths [bathe] of God, [1 Corinthians 2:10]." Everything in us that is not clean/holy He purges and burns away so we can grow into a Holy Temple [naos Holy of Holies] for A/Y who dwells in us by His Holy Spirit. [Ephesians 2:22]."

Further, in 5:24 he applies the formula above and tells of the results, "Therefore, as a tongue of fire consumes stubble, and as dry grass collapses into the flames, so the root will become like rot and their blossom blow away in dust: For, they have rejected the law [Had De Barim] of the Lord of Hosts, and have despised the Word [DeBars] of the Holy One of Israel." I had often wondered why he waited until chapter six (6) to give his revelation of the Holiness of Adonai/Yah, and this is why.

The word Adonai/Yah is explained, and we need to try to understand what they meant to Isaiah. In K&D this statement helps explain Adonai:

54

"The name Adonai is connected with the name of Jehovah for the purpose of affirming that the God of <u>salvation</u> and <u>judgment</u> has the power to carry out His promises and threats into execution." (END) 53 We have already discussed how we want the promises, but we do not believe in the threats of Deuteronomy 28:16ff, and someone has said there are three time more threats than there are blessings.

Now, I understand why he waited to chapter six (6) to tell of/about his great revelation from the Holy One of Israel. Adonai tells Isaiah, "Go, tell this people: 'Keep on listening, but do not perceive; and keep on looking, but do not understand (6:9).' " John comments about this vision in 12:41 which says "These things Isaiah said because he <u>saw</u> His Glory, and he <u>spoke</u> of Him." No, wonder Isaiah is called the Theologian and Prince of the Prophets.

Also, we know Jesus Christ used this text for His message recorded in Mark 4:12: ". . . so that while seeing, they may see and not perceive, and while hearing, they may hear and not under-stand, otherwise they may re-turn and be forgive."

This was/is not to hide the Debars/Rema Words from people, but it is to show what they/we have to understand about the Holy One of Israel. His Holiness has to be "being <u>practiced</u>" before His [DeBars/Rema] Words and Hesed [Heb] Love/Agapa [Greek] <u>can</u> be manifested in our lives. If not A/Y would be blessing our sins, and this is something that He will/cannot do, because He has provided the means of our Salvation and our Sanctification in His Debar-im/Remata Words of Jesus Christ our living Messiah.

In Isaiah 7:9 we have a repeat of Genesis 15:6 where Abram believed A/Y, and it was reckoned unto Him as righteousness. It says, "If you do

not believe, you surely will not last [concordance: be established]."
"Therefore, the Lord Himself will give you a sign: 'Behold, a virgin will
be with child and will bear a son, and she will call His name Immanuel
'God is with us.' " (7:14)

We have to go to Isaiah 9:6f to get the full understanding of this
prophecy. It says, "For a child will be born to us, a son will be given to
us; and the government will rest on His shoulders; and His [Jesus Christ]
name will be called Wonderful Counselor, Mighty God, Eternal Father,
Prince of Peace." K&D says: "The same person whom the prophet
foretold in chapter six (6), as the son of a virgin who would come to
maturity in troublous times, he here sees as born, and as having already
taken possession of the government. There he appeared as a sign, here
as a gift of Grace." (END) 54 All gifts of A/Y are of His Mercies and
Grace.

Isaiah 9:8 "sort of sums up" 7:14 and 9:6 when it says, "The Lord sends
a message [DeBar] against Jacob, and it falls on Israel." This shows the
gift of His Grace, and it is all of/by Grace through faith (Ephesians 2;
8a).

The prophets begin to make a distinction between Jacob the flesh and
Israel the faith, and if one does not make this same distinction one
cannot understand most of Paul's theology and teaching. See 1
Corinthians 10: 18, which says in Greek, "Israel according to the flesh,"
and in Romans 9:6 where he says, "not all Israel is Israel," and John's
Gospel, 1: 47b, "Behold an Israelite indeed, in whom there is no
deceit." See also: Micah 3:8: "Nevertheless, I myself am filled with
power – with the Ruach of Adonai – with judgment and with might
(geeburah = Hebrew: "manly strength") to declare (show) to Jacob his

transgression ("Pehshah" = open rebellion or a high hand) and to Israel his sin (Kat – "towarb;" "miss the mark")."

This is greatly debated and a very explosive subject, but the OT Prophets and Paul and John did state this very clearly. We can <u>deny</u> it if we want to; but when we do we will get involved in another gospel. Galatians 1:6-9 which says, "anything not of <u>faith is unrighteousness"</u> <u>"and all unrighteousnes is sin" (I John 5:17)</u>.

These passages are so profound that we will not be able to discuss them here. One must go to the commentaries to see the full impact that they have on both OT/NT Theology.

Again these passages in Isaiah are so important that we had to look at them, and now we turn back to what was said in 5:24 about the DeBar and which is repeated in 30:12-13: *"Since you have rejected this Debar and you have trust in oppression and guile, and have relied on them, Therefore this iniquity will be to you like a breach about to fall, a bulge in a high wall, whose collapse comes suddenly in a instant."* Both of these verses warn of the results of despising and rejecting the DeBars [or a seret haddebarim the ten Commandments] of A/Y which we must <u>hear</u> and <u>give</u> <u>ear</u> <u>to</u>/and <u>do</u>.

The fall of a person or a nation will come suddenly in an instant in A/Y's time as Proverbs 14:34 says: "Righteousness exalts a nation, but sin is a disgrace [reproach KJV] to any people." I have many times wondered why Solomon did not hear/do this. I think it is a <u>warning</u> to all of us that we must keep on repenting and perfecting His Holiness. When we do not obey, we cannot hear as Isaiah said in chapter 15:21: "Your ears will hear a Word [DeBar] behind you, [concordance: "Saying"] 'This is the way walk in it.' " When we reject/despise His Words [1 Samuel

15:23c] He rejects us and we lose our way and wander around like a ship without a sail.

We must listen and hear Isaiah's promising word: "A highway will be there, a roadway, and it will be called the Highway of Holiness. The unclean will not travel on it, but it will be for him/[her] who walks that way, and no fool will wander on it, But the redeemed of the Lord will walk there and the ransomed of the Lord will return, and they will be overtaken [concordance with Joy]." (Isaiah 35:9-10)

We will be giving up what 1 Peter 1: 8 says "and though you have not seen Him [Jesus Christ Messiah], you love Him, and though you do not see now, but believe in Him, you greatly rejoice with inexpressible [glorified] Joy."

This highway of Holiness is provided by [the Spirit of Holiness as it says in Romans 1:4; and 2 Corinthians 7:1], and Adonia/Yah "disciplines us for our good, so [in order that] that we may share His Holiness, [Hebrews 12:10b]." HalleluYah.

One great scholar, E. Kasemann: "Notwithstanding its use of hagiosune. It is hard to see why Paul himself would not have [used] the adjective 'Hagion' or the familiar noun 'hagiasmos?' " (END) 55

Some scholars question why Paul used this particular Greek word "hagiosunes" rather than "Hagios?" (See, 1 Thessalonians 3:13, 2 Corinthians 7:1, and Romans 1:4): These verses show that it is only used these three time in the NT and showing what it's meaning is. The **result** of Holiness is Hagiosunes while Hagomous shows the **process** of Holiness [being overtaken with Joy 39:10] by A/Y, and we have to be in the process before we can expect the Hagiosunes' result of the Holiness of Joy with A/Y.

If there can be any doubt about what it means in 1 Thessalonians 3:13, or Romans 1:4, there cannot be any doubt about how it is used in 2 Corinthians 7:1 which says, "Therefore, having all these promises, beloved, let us cleanse ourselves from all the defilement of flesh and spirit, perfecting Holiness in the fear of the God [of A/Y]." [The Greek word according to A. T. Robertson is *"Molusmos"* meaning "to pollute."] O, how much we have polluted the flesh/our Nation in America!] (END) 56

In Isaiah 39:5, 8 we have a record of a fulfilled message of the prophet Isaiah. It is "Then Isaiah said to Hezekiah, 'Hear the word of the Lord of hosts [armies].' " "Then Hezekiah said to Isaiah. 'The word of Lord which you have spoken is good.' " All A/Y Commandments /Words spoken are good [s Joshua 23:14-15]. They are all for our benefit/our good Deuteronomy 10:12.

Now, we will look at what chapters 40-66 say about the DeBars of A/Y. This second section of Isaiah is a great field to mine, and the reward will be great to anyone who does. I know all the discussion about the authors and times of it being written. I want to follow what K&D says: "It was universally assumed by both Jewish and Christian writers down to the last century, that all the canonical books of the O.T. had the **'Holy Ghost** as their one auctor primaries', and for their immediate authors the man by whose name they were called." (END) 57

Someone pointed out that for the first 500 years the Messianic believers said that the Holy Spirit wrote the Bible through Matthew, Mark, Luke, and Paul and the rest of the NT authors. It amazes me how much time and effort is put into who wrote what and not enough time trying to live out what has been written. "It stands written " as Jesus Christ says in Matthew 4:4, and as 2 Peter 3:11b "What sort of people ought you to be in holy conduct and godliness." This is all we can have any control over, and we must be doing all we can to live holy and godly lives here/now instead of trying to predict/understand all the future events.

The best discussion of the problems for some of the arguments is found in K&D, for anyone who wants to study it further. These commentators write: "These two corychcei of the modern critical school find themselves hemmed in between the two modern conclusions 'there is no true prophecy', and 'there is no true miracle.' " The greatest of all miracles is that one can be "born again from above, and **see**, and **enter** the Kingdom (John 3:3-5). When one experiences this birth from above then one does not have any problems seeing/ believing in the true prophecies and the true miracles of OT/NT.   (END)   58

K&D continues, "There is nothing strange in this great variety of ideas and forms, especially in Isaiah, who is confessedly the most universal of all the prophets." This is of no surprise because Isaiah's former life was a part of King Uzziah's government. Then, K&D: "But was Isaiah really the author of this book of consolation? Modern criticism visits all who dare to assert this with double ban of a want of science and a want of conscience." We are not trying to be scientific but we are trying to be theological, for the Bible is not about science but about Theology. (END)   59

Every time science wanders over into the field of theology it is in error because it deals with <u>what</u>/<u>how</u>. Every time theology wanders over into the field of science it is in error because it deals with <u>why</u>.

If one accepts the axiom presented by K&D - " the Holy Ghost as their one *auctor primaries*," then the science of who wrote is not as important as the fact that the Ru-ach Ha kodesh/Holy Spirit is the primary author of all the OT and all the NT.   (END) 60

We have just witnessed Nick Wallenka walking across The Grand Canyon on a wire, and the wire for the Believer across the chasm between the flesh and Spirit [Romans 8:13] is not the science of "what" or "who" but, it is the why revealed by the Ruach Ha-kodesh, and that is why we must walk in Him as we find in Galatians 5:14, 25 which says: "But I say, walk in the Spirit, and you will not carry out the desire of the flesh." ". . .and we must be being led for all who are being led ["driven" E. Kasemann] by the Spirit of God [these are the Sons/Daughters of God 2 Corinthians 6: 18b] are the sons of God, Romans 8:14," therefore, these sons/daughters are also the true Israelites John 1:47. (END)   61

As Isaiah 42:9b and Galatians 6:15-16 say, they are "a new creation" and John l:47 says, "they are without deceit" and therefore they and they only are the true Israelites.

Now, we return to our main goal of looking at the DeBars of A/Y. Isaiah 40:1 says, " 'Comfort [K&D Nachamu 'Piel literally, to cause to breathe again] ye, Comfort ye my people,' saith your God."   Not many are breathing in the H/S and/DeBars, and Isaiah 40:7c-8 gives the results "Surely the people are grass, the grass withers, the flowers fades, But the word [DeBars] of our God [A/Y] stands forever."   (END) 62

This is the great truth proclaimed about the DeBars/Debarim/A seret Hadderims of A/ Y, and if this is true, and it is, then we must know all we can about all these great Debars/ DeBarim/HadDeBarim of A/Y. Isaiah 41:26a, concludes: "Who has declared this from the beginning that we might know? Surely there was no one who declared, Surely there was no one who proclaimed, Surely there was no one who heard Your Words/DeBars, " and, this author in summing up the teaching using verses 41, 42: "We must declare, proclaim, so, that no one can say that they have not heard the Debars." Paul declares in Romans. 10:18a: "But I say, surely they have not heard, have they? Indeed they have." Indeed, all have surely heard!

CHAPTER 6

We begin to look at the Servant Songs in Isaiah 42f which is not a part of our original purpose, but it is one of the great truths or sidebars on our journey where we turn aside to <u>pause</u> and to <u>wonder</u>.

By a way of introduction we will quote from K&D: "The idea of 'a servant of Jehovah' assumed, to speak figuratively, the form of a pyramid. 'The base was Israel as a whole 41:8 [Israel as a whole was a Servant of Jehovah to serve Jehovah]; the central section was that Israel, which was not merely Israel according to the flesh, but Israel according to the Spirit also [Acts 1:8]; the apex is the person of the Mediator [Jesus Christ] of salvation springing out of Israel [John 4:22b] for salvation is out of Israel.' " (END) 63 Look where this Person was taking the Message of Jesus Christ: to the Gentiles.

Isaiah 42:1 denotes: "Behold My Servant, whom I uphold; mine elect, whom My soul loveth: I have laid My Spirit upon Him; He will bring out right to the Gentiles." A/Y upholds, ["Tamakh by" means to lay firm hold and to keep [keep hold of] upright,] [sustinere, Latin] sustained. And, I am thankful that A/Y does the upholding, and right ["Mishpat;" i.e. Absolute and therefore, Divine right; beyond the circle in which He Himself is to be found, even far away to the Gentiles.

Thanks be to Adonai/Yah that His Message to Abraham was to all nations (Genesis 17:5; Romans 4:17)! "As it is written, 'A Father of many nations have I made you.' " This shows His Divine Purpose and the Universality of A/Y's call to Abram [and to Abraham]. The rest of the Servant Songs are so prophetic and absolutely great that you must read and study them, 42:1-43:13.

Now, back to our journey of looking at the major use of the Debarim in the rest of Isaiah. In Isaiah 51:16, we have almost a NT statement about the DeBarim of A/Y which is: "I have put my word [DeBar] in your mouth and have covered you with the shadow of My Hand." O', what a great covering we have when we are covered with the shadow of His Hand, and we have the DeBars/Remata of A/Y in our mouth and in our hearts, see [Romans 10: 8 and Psalms 119:11; 'Your Debar have I treasured in my heart, that I may not sin against You'].

Not only do we not want to sin against A/Y, but we can have intimate fellowship with Him because He said ["I am watching over My Word [Debar"] ["to perform it" Jeremiah 1:12b]. The more DeBars/Remata Word we have in our mouth and on our hearts the more A/Y Watches over us with intimacy which we all desire/need. A/Y performs the "watches."

Isaiah 53 is one of the most amazing chapters in all the FC because it is like a firsthand account of a writer who is standing and witnessing the crucifixion. It was skipped over and left out of the Jewish Daily Bible reading by the Rabbi. When a Jewish believer is given this passage from Isaiah, or it is read to their parents, they think they have given them a NT book. They are startled to find it in the OT. It is being used today to witness to Jewish People all over the World. Thanks to You A/Y for the

Power of the Gospel [Ro 1:16] when we read it/preach it/teach [I Timothy 4:13f]. We are not neglecting our Charisma.

This is like the NT covenant believers who take/accept 1 Corinthians 11, which is about The Lord's Supper; then jumping over/rejecting chapter 12, which is about the Spiritual manifestation and taking/accepting chapter 13, which is about the Love of A/Y, and jumping over/rejecting chapter 14 which clearly shows how the Spiritual are to manifested in the Body [Soma] of Jesus Christ, the Messiah while they are worshipping; and then proceed to take/accept the beloved 15th chapter.   I call this "bad hop/skip theology" because 12-14 is one unit in the Greek.

Isaiah 58:13 has a very clear saying about our speaking our own debars. Note carefully,

> "IF, because of the Sabbath you turn your foot from doing your own pleasure on My Holy day, and call the Sabbath a delight, the Holy day of Lord honorable, and honor it, desisting from your own ways, from seeking your own pleasure and speaking your own word [debars]"

This verse shows how we CAN go our own way and seek our own pleasure and speak our own debars, but we will not be allowing A/Y to speak His Holy Debars in and through us.   I think Isaiah is speaking about the Sabbath rest of the NT found in Hebrews 4:9-10 which is: "So there remains a Sabbath Rest for the people of God, for the one who has entered into His Rest has himself also rested from his works, as God did from His." You can tell when a person has entered into this Sabbath Rest because he/she reflects the Glory of God at rest.   The "Hebrew "cabod" [Glory means heavy and one fall down in it"] is the visible manifestation of the invisible Kodesh [Holiness] of A/Y manifested.

Isaiah gives a vivid picture of the person who <u>can</u> and <u>will</u> be speaking the DeBars of Adonai /Yah', and it is only those described here. Let us look and listen, for A/Y is looking for a place to rest, and here it is: 66:1,2;5; where verse 1d says, "And where is a place that I may find rest?" and, Jehovah answers His own question in verse 2: "But in this one I will look, to him who is humble and contrite of spirit, and who trembles at My DeBar." Adonai/Yah does not need any rest as 40:28 says, but He is talking about a place where He can reside, reign, and be exalted as the Holy A/Y.

We need to look at these three words carefully:

- <u>humble</u> means the one who is miserable because of His/Her sins, and in whose life sin has become exceedingly sinful [Romans 7:13], and,
- <u>contrite</u> means the one that is broken hearted because of his/her sins, and,
- the one who <u>trembles</u> at A/Y Debars.

Jeremiah 23:9 illustrates this kind of Life, "As for the prophets: my heart is broken within me, all my bones tremble: I have become like a drunken man, even like a man overcome by wine, Because of the Lord and because of the Words/DeBars of His Holiness."

This is what A/Y's Debars **are**/ **do**: they are the Words of His Holiness that create and [uphold all things by the Word of His Power, Hebrews 1:3! PTL.

After we look at Micah, which is the following sidebar we go back to our journey, and continue looking at the use of the "DeBars."

We must look at Micah here, because he prophesied at about the same time that Isaiah did.

1:1 says "The word of the Lord which came to Micah," and Micah means 'Who is like the Lord?' Of course, there is none like Adonai/Yah, and I like to say and to sing: there is none **but** Adonai/Yah. HalleluYah!!!

2:7 has a beautiful message and a series of questions, which are being asked: "It is being said O house of Jacob: 'Is the Spirit of the Lord impatient'? [No! Genesis 6:3 He Strives with man.] 'Are these His doings?' [Yes.] 'Do not My words do good to the one walking uprightly?' " [Yes, Yes.] All of the questions are answered with a loud shout of "yes/yes" from the OT and the NT.

3:5f is a great sidebar for us to see the contrast between a false and true prophet. Read verse 8 and it must be quoted here: "On the other hand I am filled with power—with the Spirit of the Lord ---and with justice and courage to make known to Jacob his rebellious act, even to Israel his sin." Here is a clear distinction between **a rebellious act** [of sinning with a high hand] and even to Israel's sin as [missing the mark], which makes a clear distinction between Jacob and Israel.

In 2:7 we have the DeBars of Adonai/Yah doing good for us, and here in 3:8 His Ruach helping us to do justice and to have courage/power [Acts 1:8] to make known to Jacob his rebellious acts and to Israel his sin. So, so much for this extreme grace being preached/taught today and the false prosperity: false prophets. It is a [Hebrew a 'sheqer'] lying spirit as it says in 1Kings 22:22.

The Debar is used in 4:1-4, but it has been discussed in Isaiah already. See there . . .

I have had a revelation or revolution here. I was going on to Jeremiah, but the Spirit checked me and revealed to me that I had jumped a 100 years of Israel history. I had always tried to make this adjustment in my mind, but I had never put it down on paper, and because I am writing this paper for Bible readers and students, I needed to put it in down on paper here. The order should be: Joel 830 B.C., Jonah 825 B.C., Amos 760-740 B.C., Hosea 750 B.C., Isaiah 752-? B.C., and Micah 750-686 B.C.

To me this unscrambles the outline both for the Jewish and Messianic Believer' Bible. Before, it was like scrambled eggs, where you would try to separate the yoke from the white part after the egg is scrambled. I hope this is will be a help to all readers and students of the OT as Acts 12:25 -28:-31 is to the readers of the NT who follow the outline of Dr. A.T. Robertson in *Word Pictures of the New Testament,* of Paul's Letters in Volume 4, which unscrambles the Letters of Paul.

Thanks be to A/Y for Paul /Luke, Dr. A.T. Robertson and Dr. Dale Moody. All this is found in the NASB introduction to each book of the OT and the NT.

CHAPTER 7

Now we can turn to <u>Jeremiah</u> to learn more about the DeBars of Yahve which is used more than ninety (90) times, which shows why we can't look at all in this volume.

JEREMIAH

1: 4-12 is one of the classic statements in all the OT about the call of a prophet. It gives one of the greatest promises to all prophets who will obey the DeBars of A/Y. Verse 12 says: "Then the Lord said to me, 'You have seen well [this is what a prophet does – he **SEES**], for I am watching over My Word to perform it.' " And, all prophets have this same assurance. A/Y watches over His DeBars/Remata to protect and to perform them.

2:4 shows why the DeBar came to Jeremiah which is "Hear [that DeBar again as we must] the Word of the Lord, O house of Jacob, and all the families of the house of Israel." All the OT and the NT says it is not enough to have all the Torahs/DeBarim if we do not <u>do</u> them [in fact we are worse off [see, Amos 3:2]. Then, we are no better off than people who do not have them.

4:19 gives the anguish of Jeremiah's soul because he sees what is going to happen to Judah: "My soul, my soul! I am in anguish [A/Y cries out in the Soul/Prophet Zechariah 7:7,12]! Oh, my heart [concordance: "the walls of my heart"], my heart is pounding in me, I cannot be silent, because you [concordance: "my soul heard"] have heard; O my soul, the sound of the trumpet, the alarm of war." O', **My Soul**, we can see where America is today: as Judah was then.

5:10-13 has a stern warning to all the families of Israel. Look at verse 11: "For all the house of Israel and the house of Judah have dealt very treacherously with Me." [Jeremiah 3: 6-11, and especially verse 6-8 enlarges this thought:

> *v6 'Have you seen what faithless Israel did? She went up on every high hill and she was a harlot there,'*
> *v 7c 'but she did not return, and her treacherous sister Judah saw it',*
> *v 8 a, c 'And I saw that for all the adulteries of faithless Israel, I had sent her away and given her a writ of divorce, yet, her treacherous sister Judah did not fear; for she went and was a harlot also'].*

Why belabor this point because America has done the same thing that Israel, Judah, Rome, all Europe has done? We have a spirit of harlotry [Hosea 4:12; 9:1] also, and we think that we will not be held accountable for it, but we will as also they all were.

As Jeremiah 5:12-14 proves, "They have lied about Adonai saying, "Not He! No harm will come to us. Nor will we see sword or famine. v13 The prophets are but wind, and the word is not in them. Let what they say be done to them." v 14 Therefore, thus says Adonai Elohei-Tzva'ot:

"Because you speak this word (Debar) behold, I will make my words in your mouth fire and this people wood – and it will devour them."
Then: [15:19 explains:

> "Therefore, thus says the Lord, if you will return, then I will re store you before Me you will stand; and if you extract the precious from the worthless, you will become my spokesman [con. my mouth], and the people wood, and it will consume them".

See 23:29 also.

6:19 has a warning "Hear, O earth [O treacherous America!]: behold, I [A/Y] am bringing disaster on this people, the fruits of their plans [Isaiah 30:1b 'Who executes a plan, but not mine, and makes [pour out a drink offering] an alliance, but not of My Spirit, in order to add sin to sin; who proceed down to Egypt without consulting Me [not to consult Adonai/Yah' Ruach is to insult Him], because they have not listened to My Words [DeBars], and My Law [Torah], they have rejected it also."

This is very important because of the ruling made by our Supreme Court just recently. The secularization of American Culture and Church has been completed. We are now, (seventeen years into the 21st century, and living in a pagan society.

The cause of this can be seen clearly in Jeremiah 23:9ff: "Read, weep, and all my bones tremble; I have become like a drunken man, even like a man overcome with wine, because of the Lord and because of His Holy Words [the Words of His Holiness]." These DeBarim/Remata of A/Y are for all the peoples/Nations of the World, and we must preach and teach them to them.

Jeremiah gives His understanding of the revelation of DeBar and how it functions [29:10-14a]. He looked back over 300 years to Joshua [21:45, 23:14-15], and he saw what Joshua said about the Good DeBarim of Adonai/Yah as He quoted it.

In teaching this I asked how many of my students knew Jeremiah 29:11? Over eighty percent knew it, but not one person knew verse ten (10). You cannot have what verse eleven (11) says without having A/Y do to you what verse ten (10) says. And,

> *"So, choose life in order that you may live, you and your descendants [seed]".*
>
> *So, that all can choose Life/Blessing/live.*

Verse ten (10)(TLV) declares: "I [A/Y] will visit you, and fulfill [perform] My Good Word toward you – to bring you to this place. [Then, verse 11] 'For I [A/ Y] know the plans that I have in mind for you,' declares Adonai, 'plans for shalom and not calamity – to give a future and a hope.' " A/Y has the plan in His mind, but how do we get the plan out of His mind into our mind? I'm glad that you ask.

VV12-14a shows us how it must be done. "Then you will call on **Me**, and come and pray to **Me**, and I will listen to you. You will seek **Me** and find **Me**, when you will search for **Me** with all your Heart. Then, I [let] will be found by you." TLV

V 11 has been secularized as has Romans 8:28: "God works all things for the good," but many do not quote the rest of that verse, which says, "to them who love God, and are called according to His purpose." Now, then, God does work all thing for the good of them who love Him and are called according to His purpose, but NOT just those who "call to Him." For, instance, someone may ask God to "remove some trial." But, God is using that to fulfill His purpose in that person's life. When the person sees and learns from the trial, and embraces God's purpose in it, the prayer may be answered or the prayer may change.

So, in verse eleven (11), God does have a plan in Mind for our lives, but we must <u>Go</u>, <u>Pray</u>, and <u>Find</u> it as the Hebrew says. But rather, we make our own plans – then we ask God to bless them. Isaiah said not to consult the Ruach ha KoDesh is to insult Him. For a believer this is true, and we add sin to sin as Isaiah 30:1 says above. But, when we find His plans for our lives, He will then perform His plan and bless our lives. We will have a Hope/Future. Amen!

31:31-33 contains one of the greatest sidebars and promises in all the Holy Writ. It says, "'Behold, days are coming' declares the Lord, 'when I will make a <u>new</u> covenant with the house of Israel and the house of Judah, v 33 But this is the covenant which I will make with the house of Israel after those days', declares the Lord, 'I will put My law [Torahs] within them and on their heart. I will write it; and I will be their God, and they shall be My people." This has been fulfilled in the new covenant as is shown in 2 Corinthians 6: 14-7:1:

> *14 Do not be unequally yoked with unbelievers.[c] For what partnership is there between righteousness and lawlessness? Or what fellowship does light have with darkness? 15 What harmony does Messiah have with Belial[d]? Or what part does a believer have in common with an unbeliever? 16 What agreement does God's Temple have with idols?[e] For we are the temple of the living God—just as God said,*

73

"I will dwell in them and walk among them;
and I will be their God,
and they shall be My people.[f]
[17] *Therefore, come out from among them,*
and be separate, says ADONAI.
Touch no unclean thing.[g]
Then I will take you in.[h]
[18] *I will be a father to you,*
and you shall be My sons and daughters,
says ADONAI-Tzva'ot."[i]

*{7:1} Therefore, since we have these promises, loved ones, let us
cleanse ourselves from all defilement of body and spirit, perfecting
holiness in the fear of God.* TLV

Jeremiah 37:3-4, 17, tells the story of what happened to Jeremiah. "Yet King Zedekiah sent Jehucal the priest, to Jeremiah the prophet, saying, 'Please pray to the Lord our God on our behalf.' v4 Now, Jeremiah was still coming in and going out among the people, for they had not yet put him in prison." They needed his prayers, and later in verse 17 Zedekiah secretly asked of him and said, " 'Is there a Word [DeBar] from the Lord?' and Jeremiah said '<u>There</u> [there always is a living DeBar/Rema from the Living A/Y i.e. Ps 19:4; Ro 10:18] <u>is</u>!' Then he said, 'You will be given into the hand of the king of Babylon!' " Judah had rejected A/Y [DeBars] Words and His 'a seret had Debarim' Torahs. Therefore, they were going into captivity as the penalty for the rejection, as all do who reject the DeBar of A/Y.

Lamentations is sort of a wailing of Jeremiah because he had witnessed the fall of Jerusalem, and the burning of the Temple in 586 B. C. The prophet got no joy out of seeing Jerusalem fall, and the Temple burned because He believed that A/Y had a plan in mind for His People: " 'For I know the plans that I [concordance: "am planning for you"], have for you,' declares the Lord, 'plans for welfare and not calamity to give you a future/ a hope.' " (Jeremiah 29:11 TLV) Even in A/Y wrath [Romans 1:18] A/Y is planning a future/ hope for His Israel: **His special treasure.**

In 2:14-19 he says, "Your prophets have seen for you false and foolish visions and they have not exposed your iniquity." This proves that the prophecy of Jeremiah about Israel going into Babylonian captivity was true. The false prophets said those in exile would be back soon (Jeremiah 20:4). Your prophets are preaching their false doctrines and false foolish vision of prosperity, rather than exposing your/ our sins/iniquities. v17 "The Lord has done what He purposed; He has accomplished His Word [DeBar] which He commanded from day of old. He has thrown down without sparing, and He has caused the enemy to rejoice over you; He had exalted might [con. horn] of your adversaries." A/Y purposed: in Deuteronomy 30:1a, 19:

> *"I have set before you today life and prosperity [concordance: "good"] and death and adversity [evil],*
>
> *v 19 'I call heaven and earth to witness against you today, that I have set before you life and death, the blessing and the curse. So, choose life in order that you may live, you and your descendants [seed]."*

So, that all can choose Life/Blessing/live.

In **Chapter Eight** we will consider the work of Ezekiel. According to the intro in NASB, the prophet Ezekiel was among the more than 3,000 Jews exiled to Babylon. He was a priest and he had a calling to become a prophet while in bondage.

CHAPTER 8

And now we can follow the outline, and look at **Ezekiel.** The name Ezekiel means "God is strong," and, what a message for a people in bondage/Babylon.

Von Rad says, "We may therefore start by supposing that Ezekiel arrived in Babylon with the deportation in 598 B.C., that he was there called to be a prophet in 593 B.C, and that he exercised his office until 571 B.C." (END) 64   This gives us the date/time that he prophesied.

1:3 says "The word [DeBar] of the Lord came expressly to Ezekiel the priest, by the river Chebar; and there the hand of Lord came upon him." This may be where Paul got the information of   1 Timothy 4:1 [G. Now the Spirit says expressively in words], and it shows that <u>with</u> <u>DeBar</u>

> *Ezekiel gives us a deep look into the heart of God!*

<u>came</u> the hand [<u>the</u> <u>anointing</u>] of the Lord. The people answered A/Y that they would do what A/Y said to do and what He speaks to them **through** His Prophets.

3:16f, illustrates how and what the prophet is to do: "At the end of seven days the word of the Lord came to me, saying, 'Son of Man, I have appointed you a watchman to the house of Israel; whenever you hear a word from My mouth, warn them for Me,' " and, this is repeated in 33:7: "I have appointed you a watchman for the house of Israel; so you will hear a message [DeBar] from My mouth: give them warning for Me."

This is it: it has to be a DeBar/ Remata from the mouth of A/Y or it is not a Living Word of the Living A/Y which warns them for Him. Man cannot break/ bind/release/destroy it: it must be a word **[DeBars/Remata] from** A/Y's Mouth to have the anointing which performs the Miracles. Most of the DeBars in Ezekiel are: the Debar came to me from A/Y mouth.

11:23-25 has a great sidebar and a discussion about the Glory [Kadosh of Adonai/Yah]. It says:

> *The Glory of the Lord went up from the midst of the city and stood over the mountain which is east of the city, v24 and the Spirit lifted me up and brought me in a vision by the Spirit of God to the exiles in Chaldea [Babylon]. So, the vision that I had seen left [went up from] me, v25 Then I told the exiles all the things that the Lord had shown me."*

". . . the Glory of A/Y is not limited to the Temple . . . but . . . will be with the People of A/Y wherever they are: . . ."

This shows that the Glory of A/Y was/is not limited to the Temple in Jerusalem, but that it will be with the People of A/Y wherever they are: in the exile in Babylon which brought great comfort to the people then, and now, when any believer is in exile [see:1 Corinthians 3:16-17, 6:19-20; 2 Corinthians 6:16].

12:25 gives us a deep look into the heart of A/Y which says, "For I the Lord will speak, and whatever Word I speak will be performed. It will no longer be delayed, for in your days, O rebellious house, I will speak the Word and <u>perform</u> it, <u>declares</u> the Lord God." A/Y has/does!!!

One of the best known passages in all Ezekiel is in Chapter 37. So, Adonai/Yah shows the prophet that Israel was like dry bones. There bones were very dry. There was no life in these very dry bones. Adonai/Yah says to Ezekiel, " 'Son of man, can these dry bone live again?' And I answered, 'O God [concordance: "YHWH"] You know.' " Verse four (4) continues, "Again He said to me, 'Prophesy over these bones and say to them, "O dry bones, hear the word [Debars] of the Lord.' ' " If there is any hope for the American modern day secularized Church she will have to hear the DeBars/Remata of the Living A/Y, and allow Him to revive these very dry bones and to perform these DeBarim in and through Her.

Verse 11 explains the vision, "Then He said to me, 'Son of man, these bones is the whole house of Israel; behold they say, "our bones are dried up and our hope has perished. We are completely [concordance: "cut off to ourselves"] cut off." ' " This is so true when Israel or we reject Adonai/Yah DeBarim - we are cut off to ourselves, and even when He is correcting us there is a revelation of His salvation in His Wrath.

Von Rad says, "But another thing which makes the prophets' proclamation something absolutely <u>new</u> and hitherto <u>unheard of</u> in Israel was that, even in the very act of proclaiming judgement, they made known the beginnings of a new movement toward salvation." (END) 65 This new movement fulfilled, included, and perfected the old with something better, for if it did not then it would be more than the prophet could stand. It is all he can do to see A/Y's wrath poured out on disobedient Israel or the Messianic believers. See Romans 1:18f, where it says that His wrath is being poured out from Heaven/not from hell on all ungodliness in the world and unrighteousness in the Messianic Body/Soma.

Now we will look at **Habakkuk** which does not have any DeBarim in it, but does have some important information about the living oracles of Adonai/Yah.

1:4 says, "There the law is ignored [concordance: "numbed"] and justice is [never goes forth] never upheld. For the wicked surround the righteous; therefore justice comes out perverted." Isaiah has an insight into this in 5:20a where it says, "Woe to those who call evil good, and good evil." This warning sounds like it is the warning to the modern world and America, but we will be held accountable for our sins just as Israel and Judea was/is.

1:5 has a great warning oracle which says "Look among the nations! Observe! Be astonished! Wonder! Because I [A/Y] am doing something in your day – you would not believe if you were told." This sounds just like something that Adonai/Yah is doing today in His world. This passage was quoted in Acts 13:16f, in Paul's first missionary sermon in Pisidian, Antioch and Paul was commenting upon the conditions in Pisidian Antioch, and he uses the same as quoted above.   In verse 40:   "Therefore, take heed, so that the thing spoken of in the Prophets may not come upon you: v41 Behold, you scoffer, and marvel, and perish [concordance: "disappear"]." Listening to all the serious warning in both passages, and it makes one wonder how we can ignore the same warning today in our world; and sadly in the secularized Church in America?

3:1-2: "A prayer of Habakkuk the prophet, according to the Shigionoth [concordance: "a highly emotional poetic form"] v 2 'Lord, revive Your work in the midst of the years, in the midst of the years make it known; in wrath remember mercy [concordance: "Compassion"]' " This shows how the true prophet cries out in his/her heart to Adonai/Yah for His people. His/Her prayer is always for Adonia/Yah to have mercy /compassion upon His people and to revive them.

Psalms 85:7 has a great insight into the word "revive" which is - "Will You not Yourself revive [concordance: "generation and generation"] us again, that Your People may rejoice in You?" A/Y creates/generates us, and then He has to regenerate us by continuously sanctifying us through the Spirit and Word.

Hebrew 2:11 says in Greek "For both the [One] sanctifying and the one being sanctified [are] all of One." Oh, to be One with the Ruach ha KODESH /Remata Words for, it says in 1 Timothy 4:6 "For it is sanctified by the means of the Word of God and prayer." Read/Pray for Revival.

Now, we will look at **Haggai** which I did not see before, but Adonai/YHWH gave me an insight on it. It proves what I have been saying since 1970, that we cannot speak the DeBar/Rema words. They must be spoken **through** us by the Ruach haKo-desh, as it says in Haggai I:I, 3; 2:1. It says "the Word [DeBar] of Adonai'YHWH came **through** Haggai], in all three places.

In 2:5 it says, 'According to the word' [The Hebrew says "eth-Had-dabhar"] I [Adonai/YHWH] **covenanted with you when you came out of Egypt. My Ruach is remaining/standing in your midst. Do not fear."**

K&D says, "The Word 'eth-Had-dabhar' which the Lord concluded with Israel when He led it out of Egypt, can only be the promise which established the covenant, to the fulfillment of which God [YHWH] Himself in relation to the people, when He led them out of Egypt, namely, the word that He would make Israel into His own property out of **all** nations Exodus 19:5-6."   (END) 66   Consider the words "for **all** nations" a moment. Genesis 12:2-3; 17:5. This looks back unto Moses in about 1200 B.C. and ties all the DeBarim together. So, what YHWH did in 1250 B.C. He was still doing in 580 B.C. and He is still doing according to Acts 7:38, because they **were** and **are** living oracles[NT = logi] today. And they are still living Debarim/Remata Words of Adonai/YHWH which we are supposed to be preaching and teaching today.   [see Romans 10:8]

HalleluYah! No wonder Paul was so happy that Adonai/ YHWH considered him worthy to be entrusted with and to preach /teach the glorious Gospel (1 Timothy1:11-12). HalleluYah be to our Holy/Living/Adonai/YHWH.

<u>Zachariah</u> means "The Lord remembers," and He is trying to get Judea to remember in verse six (6). "But did not My Words and My statutes, which I commanded overtake your fathers? Then they repented." Oh, A/Y let Your Words and Torahs overtake the World and America and the Messianic body of Jesus Christ today so they/we will repent!!!

V13 says, "The Lord answered the angel who was speaking with me with gracious [concordance: "Good"] words, comforting words."

This is what the DeBars/Re-mata Words [Gracious/Comforting Words] of A/Y are doing! But we cannot have "This Love and Peace" without hearing and doing His Words. 2 Corinthians 13:11 in the Greek says, *"Finally, brethren, rejoice, <u>be</u> perfected, <u>be</u> comforted, <u>be</u> of one mind, <u>be</u> in peace and live in peace; and the God of [Hebrew Hesed Love/Greek Agape Love] Love and Peace will be with you."*

<u>THIS IS IT</u>: A/Y Words has to be being perfected in us and be given to others in love or there is no peace. This is the only verse in the NC that Dr. A.T .Robertson, in all his writing, did not somewhere translate, and give the correct Greek translation of it, as above.

It teaches that we are to be perfected like Paul said in Philippians 3:12, "Not that I have already obtained it or have already become prefect [have been perfected is a pass perfect in Greek which means that it was not finished in the pass, but it must be going on continuously in the presence: Marshall in his literal translation], but I press on so [con. If I may even] that I may lay hold of that for [concordance: "Because also"] which also I was laid hold of by Christ Jesus."

This interpretation above is proven by verse 15, which says, "Let us therefore, as many as are perfect, have this attitude; and if in anything you have a different attitude, God will reveal that also to you; v16 however, let us keep living [concordance: Following in line] by that same standard to which we have attained." These two subjectives let us know and shows to us what we must be doing. Let us be walking in line with what has been revealed to us, and if we are not, then nothing new can be being revealed to us because we are not walking in what has already been revealed to us/period.

4:6 has an awesome message: "Then He said to me [concordance: "said to me saying"], 'This is the Word [Debar] of the Lord to Zerubbabel' saying, 'Not by might, nor by power, but by My Spirit', says the Lord of Hosts.' " This is such a revealing passage from A/Y that we have to pay close attention to it because we think we have such great power and might that we are right.

Jeremiah 20: 10 says, "For the land is full of adulterers; for the land mourns because of the curse. The pastures of the wilderness have dried up. Their course also is evil, and their might is not right." I was going to quote just the last sentence in this verse, but the whole verse reveals the condition in the world and in America and sadly in Church today.

6:8 has a profound statement as expressed in the TLV: "Then He called and spoke to me saying, 'Look! Those going toward the land of the north:' "

K&D says: Let down My Ruach [HaDodesh] in the North." This is what all believers filled with the Rauch HaKodesh are to do. We are to be

84

letting down His Divine Ruach HaKodesh in everything we say or wherever we go.

Now, we can look at 7:7, where we find an interpretation of what Adonai/Yah does in the life of His prophets. "Are not these the Words [Debarim] which the Lord proclaimed [hath cried, Hebrew] by the mouth of the former prophets when Jerusalem was inhabited and prosperous [at ease] along with the cities around it, and the Negev [south country] and the foothill were inhabited?" I was so blown away with this passage that I had to rest and to pray and to search/research for a day before I could comment on it.

For it shows how that America has been at ease since the end of the World War II, because of the prosperity, while A/Y has been crying and trying to find prophets through whom He could cry out. The secularized Church in the world and

> *America has been at ease since the end of the World War II, because of the prosperity . . .*

In America is <u>at</u> <u>ease</u>. O, Abba, A/Y forgive us and revive us according to the Word [Psalm 119:25] again in the name of Jesus Christ our Saviour and Lord, I pray.

7:12 also sounds like a New Testament passage which is: "They made their hearts like flint from [hearing] the Torah and the words [DeBarim] which Yahve of Hosts [Armies] had sent by His Spirit through the former prophets; therefore great wrath came from the Yahve of Hosts." This is repeated in Romans 1:18f where the wrath comes from heaven [not hell] upon all ungodliness in the world/all unrighteousness of the righteous. 1 John 5:17 says: "It's sin."

<u>Malachi</u> 1:1 [means "My Messenger"] "The oracles [concordance: "burden"] of the word [DeBarim] of the Lord to Israel through Malachi."

Jeremiah has already warned about calling the Word of the Lord a burden – in Jeremiah 23:33: "Now when this <u>people</u> or the <u>prophet</u> or a <u>priest</u> [Pastors] asks you saying 'What is the oracle [burden] of the Lord? Then you shall say to them 'What oracle [burden]?' The Lord declares. 'I will abandon you.' " Verse 36 says, "For you will no longer remember the oracle [burden] of the Lord, because man's own word will become the oracle [burden], and you have perverted the Words [Debars] of the living God, the Lord of hosts, and our God." His DeBars/ Remata are not a burden but a great <u>blessing</u> of A/Y - As we will see now as we look at Psalms.

CHAPTER 9

Now, we come to the Book of **Psalms** which covers a period of over eleven hundred years, beginning with Moses: *The Songs of Israel.* I was hurrying to get to Psalms and Adonai/ Yah through the Spirit said to me, "Billy, slow down and pray, and do some research." I did and here is what I found.

Israel became a Singing and Worshiping People – Semitic people who worshipped all kinds of gods. They mingled their worship with El, elohim/Baalism; and, Adonai/Yah when He brought them up out of Egypt through Moses. Exodus 19:5 describes it this way: "And, how I bore you on eagles' wings, [the Hebrew Ruach hakodesh/Gr. Hagios Pneumata: wings the early symbol of the Spirit] and, brought you to Myself." This historical event is recorded in Deuteronomy 4: 32-38: "Because He loved your Fathers, therefore He chose their descendants [his seed Gal 3:16] after them. And He [concordance: "with His presence" { 'K& D By His <u>Face</u>' }] brought you from Egypt with great <u>Power;</u>" and, further, as we see in Exodus 15:1-20 which says: "Then Moses and the sons of Israel sang this song to the Lord ; and said, [concordance: "saying: ' <u>Let me/ us</u> <u>sing</u> <u>to the</u> <u>Lord</u>' "] I will sing to the Lord, for He [has triumphed gloriously]; the horse and its rider He has hurled into the sea;" v 21 "Miriam [the prophetess, v 20] answered them [Moses and the sons of Israel, and this is where the Israelite dance began] 'Sing to the Lord for He [has triumphed gloriously]; the horse and his rider He has hurled into the sea.' "

This is confirmed in Hosea 13: 9a: "But I [Adonai/Yah] have been the Lord your God since Egypt." Has He become your Adonai/Yah yet? [1 Peter 3:15a commands everyone to: ". . . sanctify Christ {not God as KJV says} in your hearts as Lord?"]   You/We must sanctify Christ as A/Y Lord here and now, because we are the Living Body of Christ!!

This is done by letting Adonai/Yah sanctify us. Exodus 31:13d verifies: ". . .that you may know that I am the Lord [Adonai/Yah] who sanctifies you." PT

We must sanctify Christ as A/Y Lord here and now, because we are the Living Body of Christ!!

The songs and the singing, and the dancing was/is on, and it has been ever since the Sons of Adonai/Yah and of Israel sang [Romans 8:14]. Let us sing for [Adonai/Yah has triumphed gloriously] in the Jewish believers, and in the Messiah, and in the Messianic body [soma] of Him.

I had always thought that the first part of Psalms was written by David. I found out that there are five books in Psalms: I-41; 42-72. These first two were written by David and the remaining three were written by others: 73-89; 90-106; and 107-150. It says in Psalm 72:20 "The prayers of David the son of Jesse are ended." I was surprised that it said prayers rather than Psalms, but "'all spiritual songs' are prayers Ephesians 5:19a." That is why we must pray in the Spirit. We see in Ephesians 6:18a-b "Marshall', in Greek gives the meaning: "by means of all prayer and petition, praying at every [concordance says: "pray without ceasing see;" 1 Thessalonians 5:17] time in Spirit," and Jude 20. Read and memorize it.

We are looking at the use of the DeBars, and we will pass over many wonderful passages in Psalms. The first appearance is in Psalms 5:1, "Give ear to my words" [DeBars is used as David words] O, Lord, consider my groaning [concordance: "meditations"]. I like the way David used this word, because it shows that Adonai/Yah does hear our groaning/our meditations. That is why he used DeBar as his prayer/so should we.

12:6 gives a very beautiful picture of the DeBars when David declares: "The Words [Debars] of the Lord are pure Words, as silver tried in a furnace on the earth refined seven times." That is **pure** silver, and these are **the pure** Debars of Adonai/Yah which will purify us as His Temple, [Greek Naos the Holy of Holiest, see: 1 Corinthians 3:16] if we allow Him.

18:30 has a beautiful title which I had never read until now as I look at the DeBars in it, and that is why we must study these DeBars. The title says: "To the chief Musician, a Psalm of David, the servant of the Lord, who spake unto the Lord, these words [Debars] of this song in the day that the Lord delivered him from the hand all his enemies, and from the hand of Saul." Psalms 107:2 admonishes us, "Let all the redeemed of Adonai/Yah say so, whom He hath redeemed from the hand of the enemy." Hallelujah let us say so.

He said in v 30: "As for God, His way is blameless [complete, having integrity, or perfect]; the Word of the Lord is tried." His Torah and His words [DeBars] have been tried, and both have been founded to be faithful, complete, or having integrity, and perfect. So, when someone says that Adonai/Yah Torah and DeBars, are not perfect, then we know that they do not know the Living Adonai/Yah, nor His Living Debarim/Remata.

33:3-5 is such a blessing to me, because it says: "Sing to Him a new song; play skillfully with a shout of Joy [If you personally know me then you now know why I shout so much.] v 4 For the Word of the Lord is upright [and it will make us upright if we allow it], and all His work is done in faithfulness. v5 He [Adonai/Yah] loves righteousness and justice." [So, He still loves America but He does not love the unrighteousness or injustice in America.

. . .the reason that I use Adonai/Yah [is]because it is using the Hebrew Words for God and not the Semitic El/Elohim.

Isaiah 5:7: "For the vineyard of the Lord of hosts is the house of Israel, and the men of Judah His delightful plant. Thus He looks for justice, but behold bloodshed; for righteousness, but behold a cry of distress"; the earth is full of the Lovingkindness [used 640 times in the OT] of the Lord. v6 By the Word [Debar] of the Lord the heaven were made, and by the breath of His Mouth their hosts."

Isaiah 49:6 says, "He [Adonai/Yah] says, 'It is no small thing that you should be My Servant to raise up the tribes of Jacob and to restore the preserved ones of Israel; I will also make you a light of [to] the nations so that My salvation may reach to the end of the earth.' " This has always been Israel assignment to bring salvation, righteousness, and justice to the end of the earth, and now it is the assignment of the Messianic Body of Jesus Christ, "our Messiah" to <u>do</u> it.

And it is only by His Power [Acts 1:8] that we can accomplish any of the above tasks which is confirmed by Hebrews I:3b "and uphold [concordance: "in"] all things by the Word [Rema] of His Power." The Greek says in Marshall "and Bearing all things by the Word [DeBar] of His Power." That word bearing is so important because it is used in 2 Peter 1: 21 where it says in Marshall again, "No, not by the will of man prophecy was borne [bear] <u>at</u> <u>any</u> <u>time</u>, but being borne by the Holy Spirit, men spoke from God." If men/women are not being borne [carried] along by the Holy Spirit they cannot be prophesying or speaking any of the living DeBars/Remata of the living A/Y.

56:5 is a good place to discuss the difference between the Hebrew verses and the English verses. In the Hebrew, verse one in the TLV says "For the Leader. Set to 'The Silent Dove of the Distance.' By David; a mikhtam when the Philistines captured him in Gath' " which is recorded in 1 Samuel 21:10f. I/We have a lot to learn about the Psalms and about the whole first OT and NT.

The TLV says in 56:4 "Most High, when [NASB "In the Day"] I am afraid, I will put my trust in you. In God—I praise His Word [Debar]—In God I trust; I have no fear; what can human power do to me?" Verse ten (10) has: "In God, whose Word I praise-whose word I praise twice."

In the day that I am afraid I will put my trust in A/Y and His Debars. This is the reason that I use Adonai/Yah because it is using the Hebrew Words for God and not the Semitic El/Elohim.

Psalm 105:19f is a good example of how the Debar works if we wait, and sometime we have to wait for it to be fulfilled. v19 "Until the time that his word came to pass; the word of the Lord tested [refined] him [Joseph]." What is so important about this is that until the time "that His word came to pass?" The DeBarim of the A/Y tested or refined Joseph: He must test/refine us!

Sometime the Lord has to test/refine us before we are to see the fulfillment of the DeBars that A/Y has spoken / speaks unto us. v 18 explains what happened to Joseph before His Word came to pass, "They afflicted his feet with fetters, and he himself [concordance: "His soul came into irons"] was laid in irons," and so our soul needs to come into iron. Sometimes the test is given so that we will have a testimony when the DeBar does come to pass. HalleluYah!!

In 105: 26-27 we have a profound message about the DeBarim which says "He [A/Y] sent Moses and Aaron, whom He had chosen, And they set [NASB] His signs---miracle among in the land of Ham." This explains that we must be sent and we must set the DeDarim/ Remata Words of A/Y among the people and they must believe them [the words of A/Y go on working if we go believing 1 Thessalonians 2:13c] before the Signs/ Wonder/Miracle can be performed in Us/Through Us.

Isaiah 40:31 illustrates this principle: "Yet those who wait [concordance: "hope in"] for the Lord will gain new strength; they will mount up [concordance: "sprout wings"] with wings [pinions] like eagles, they will run and not get tired, they will walk and not become weary." Let our soul become like iron so we want become weary.

The result is well worth the wait, as Habakkuk 2:2-3 says: when the vision [Debar] tarries wait for it:

> "Then the Lord answered me and said, 'record the vision and inscribe it on tablets, that the one [one may read it fluently] who reads [is to proclaim it] it may run. v3 For the vision is yet for the appointed time; it hasten [concordance: "pants"] toward the goal and it will not fail [lie]. Though it tarries, wait for it; for it will certainly come to pass."

This happened to me from 1970, when I received the baptism of the Holy Spirit as it says in Luke 3:15. I had asked and prayed to A/Y for some young people whom I could mentor in all that I had learned about the Holy Spirit. My prayers were answered in 2010 when I met again Jason Thomley and through him met Todd Hunt. These last seven years have been the most blessed and wonderful years of my life. As stated above, after learning about the DeBars and finding Eichrodt info in his book, since March 19, 2013, about the DeBarim – it has been like putting the icing on the cake of my whole life. HalleluYah to Adonai/Yah!!!!!!

106:12 gives a studied contrast between itself and v 24. Verse 12 says "Then they believed His Words; they sang His Praises." This shows what we are to do. We are to believe His DeBarim and sing His praises.

. . . if we go believing . . . Signs/ Wonders/Miracles can be performed in Us/Through Us . . .

27:6 declares "And now my head will be lifted up above my enemies around me, and I will offer in His tent sacrifices with [concordance: "shouts of Joy"] Joy." Shouting sacrifices of Joy are offered in His tent/house of Holiness.

v 24-25 shows the very opposite: "Then they despised the pleasant land: they did not believe in His Word, but grumbled in their tents; they did not listen to the voice of the Lord." This is taken from Numbers 14:1-2: *"Then all the congregation lifted* [concordance: "utter and gave their voice"] *their voice and cried, and the people wept that* [concordance: "in that night"] *night. All the sons of Israel grumbled against Moses and Aaron; and the whole congregation said to them 'would that we had died in the land of Egypt!' "* This is how grumbling [see Psalms 37:1-8] gives Satan the opportunity to discourage us in our time of testing.

Sometime Adonai/Yah wants to see if we really mean business with Him when we are asking for His Blessing/His Debars for ourselves and other. We cannot despise His DeBars and receive His Blessing/DeBars.

107:20 is often quoted without the context of 17-22 which gives a correct meaning to the DeBar. We must have the correct text, context, or we will have <u>pretext</u>. Verse 17 says the "Fools, because of their rebellious way, and because of iniquities, were afflicted; v 19 Then they cried out to the Lord [Adon-ai/Yah] in their trouble; He saved them out of their distresses. V 20 He sent His word [DeBar] and healed them, and delivered them from their destructions [Hebrews: 'pits']."

<u>Here</u> was another check by the Holy Spirit because I had moved on to Psalm 119, but in the night He said I needed to go back and take a closer look, so I did and this is what I found.

Exodus 15: 26 has the famous quote ["I am Yahve thy healer!" {Yahve' rapher}] that is quoted all the time, but again the context of 15:22-26 must be looked at because it gives the correct meaning and interpretation. v26 "And He said 'if you will give earnest <u>heed</u> to the voice of the Lord your God, and <u>do</u> what is right in His sight, and give <u>ear</u> to His commandment [A seret HadDebarim], and all His statutes, I will put none of the diseases on you which I have put up-on the Egyptians: for I, the Lord , am your healer."

It is true in Psalms 107:20, it is true in Exodus 15: 26, and it is true in James 5:13f. "Is anyone among you suffering? Then he must pray. Is anyone cheerful? He is to sing praises. v14 Is anyone among you sick? Then he must call for the elders of the church and they are to pray over him, anointing [having anointing] him with oil in the name of the Lord; 15 and the prayer offered [of] in faith well restore [save] the one who is sick, and the Lord will raise him up, and if he has committed sins, they [it] will be forgiven him. v16 Therefore, confess your sins one to another and pray for one another so that [Greek: "so as"] you may be healed, a petition of a righteous man being made effective much [very] is strong."

The real clincher is in 1 Peter 2:24 "And He Himself bore [concordance: "carried...up to the cross"] our sins in His own body on the cross, so that [in order that = "a purpose clause" my commentary] we might die to sin [sins: KJV got it right because he is talking about sanctification my commentary] and live unto righteousness; [by His wounds we were healed from sins unto righteousness my commentary]." I don't see how it could be any clearer that Peter is talking about being healed from our sins...our soul being healed...[soul healing has been my calling since I have received the Holy Spirit in 1970 because for everyone who needs healing in their body I have met ten who needed healing in their soul...] our sanctification, HalleluYah. Not just our physical healing which happen many times when our soul is healed: He [Restoreth my/[our] soul Psalm 23:3].

I don't understand how some are healed and some are not. But, I know that whenever anyone is healed and they are; it is Adonai/Yah who does the healing, and not some so called faith healer. I have learned a great deal by looking at all these verses together, and I hope that you want to learn/know the truth taught in Adonai/Yah' Holy [Scriptures Romans 1: 2] Words!!!

CHAPTER 10

Now, we will look at Psalm 119 which shows the classical use of DeBar in the OT, and it is one of the most important sections in the Psalms. It also gives a full picture of the uses/meaning of the DeBars. I have only chosen those verses that give the different shades of the meaning to the DeBarim here and all the way through the OT.

The Psalmist asks "How can a young [all men and women] man keep his way pure? By keeping it according to Your Word." When we seek /keep it with all our hearts. v10 "With all my heart I have sought You; do not let me wander from your commandments [a seret Haddebarim]. v11 "Your word I have treasured in my heart, that I may not sin against You" (Psalm 119:9-11). But, we can have fellowship with You as You watch over your Word to perform it, Jeremiah 1: 12].

O' dear, A/Y, help us to hide all your words in our mind that we can, in order that the Holy Spirit may write [2 Corinthians 3:3 "written not with ink but with the Spirit of the Living God"] them on our hearts: your living Debar/Rema.

Psalm 119:25, 28: "My soul cleaves to the dust; Revive me according to Thy DeBar." This shows us how we can and must be revived. I have prayed and heard so many people pray for revival; but nothing happened and now I know why because we had not been revived according to A/Y's [Debarim/Remata] Words.   v93 agrees with this concept "I will never forget Your precepts [a seret Haddebarim]. For by them You revived me."

Then, verse 28 says: "My soul weeps [drops] because of grief; strengthen me according to Thy Word." My soul is weeping [dropping] because of all the grief and misery in my flesh and that is in Your world today. I thank You A/Y for your longsuffering with Israel and the Messianic Body of Jesus Christ and **me**, and that your Hesed/Agape are holding back your wrath [Romans 2:4b forbearance (anoeches, old word, holding back from anoecho)] that is only used here in the NT.

In A.T. Robertson we find: "holding back Your Wrath by your Hesed/Agape Love," (END)   67   and I guess that it will always be that way until Your return, and, until You wipe away all the

tears and pain that is in us and Your World [see Revelation 21: 4]. Psalm 119:41 A/Y teaches us how this is done: "May Your loving kindnesses also come to me, O Lord, Your salvation according to your Word." And, verse 77 further explains this lovingkindness: "May your compassion [tender mercies, KJV] come to me that I may live, for Your law is my delight." If His Torah and DeBars are our delight, then we will be continuously being revived in spite of all our suffering and misery. Psalm 119:47 reveals the secret: "I shall delight [concordance: "delight myself"] in Your commandments [A secret HadDebarim] which I Love." This is the only way that we will ever stop sinning – when we Love His Presence/Commandments more than we love our sins. In Exodus 20:20 it says, "Moses said to the people, 'Do not be afraid; for God has come in order to <u>test</u> you, and in order that the fear of Him may remain [concordance: "be before"] with you, so that you may not sin.' "

This is it! We have to love A/ Y more that we love our sins, or we will **not** stop sinning. This is where Paul got his teaching found in 2 Corinthians 7:1. "Therefore having all these promises, beloved, <u>let us</u> cleanse ourselves *[present active subjunctive, something that we have to do with the help of the H/S]* from all defilement of flesh and spirit, perfecting Holiness in the . . . fear of the Lord." The Augsburg Confession, "presented June 25, 1530, in German and Latin at the Diet of Augsburg to the emperor Charles V by seven Lutheran princes. . ." says, "Protestant perfection is the perfection of repentance in the fear of the Lord," [3] and, I would add: "perfecting of repentance" and "perfecting Holiness." Back to 2 Corinthians 7:1: "in the fear of the Lord." We have to perfect 'repentance', before we can be perfecting 'His Holiness.' "The fear of the A/Y is his/[our] treasure Isaiah 33:6c." So that, when we sin against A/Y: we confess it immediately." Confessing of our sins as James 5:16 says, will give us our soul and body healing/Peace. P.T.L.

In 1 Corinthians 15:34, Paul says, "Become sober minded [righteously as A.T. Robertson points out 'Awake up righteously, Wake up [and stop sinning'] as you ought and stop sinning; for some have no knowledge of God. I speak this to your shame." (END) 68   It is a shame that so many in the Messianic Body [Soma of Jesus Christ] today, take sin so lightly, but Paul said in Romans 7:13, the last phrase: "so that through the commandments ['A seret Haddebarim'] sin would become exceedingly sinful." Help us to see what sin is/ does to our human

---

[3] https://www.britannica.com/topic/Augsburg-Confession

soul/body, and to Your Messiah [soma]. No wonder the world has no clear concept of what sin is and does, because the Body of Messiah is giving such mixed messages about sin! Some, so called preachers don't use the word "sin" any more. They use the word mistake/fault rather than sin. A/Y help us to hear Your Holy Debars/Rameta and STOP sinning.

Psalm 119:50 has a beautiful message, and it is: "My comfort in my affliction is this: Your Word has kept me alive." My daughter was in the hospital in Atlanta, and I was praying and asking Jesus Christ for a Word, and He gave me verse 50. What a great wonderful promise/blessing.

The supreme court of the United States of America (or any nation – added by editor) is not the Supreme Court of Heaven. Sin may be made legal by man's ruling on earth, but it is still illegal by Adonai!

However, verse 67 gives a warning and a blessing: "Before I was afflicted I went astray, but now I keep your Word." When will we believers realize that our afflictions and harassment are for OUR GOOD [Jeremiah 9:11 as noted above], and they only happen when we keep on keeping the DeBarim/Remata Words? Coupled with that is a great affirmation in verse 74: "May those who fear [concordance: "revere"] You see me and be glad, because I wait [concordance: "hope in"] for Your Word." It seems that we are not able to see another who has hoped in God's Word like we should, and we make the same mistakes without learning from them by not hoping in the Living Words.

Psalm 119:89 says, "Forever, O Lord [O, A/Y], Your Word [DeBar, Debarim, and A seret HaddeBarim] is [concordance: "Stands firm"] settled in heaven." The supreme court of the USA is not the Supreme Court of Heaven. Sin may be made <u>legal</u> by man's ruling on earth, but it is still <u>illegal</u> by Adonai/Yah' Supreme Moral ruling Court in Heaven.

We <u>must</u> make the decision by which ruling we are going to abide, and live our lives; for if we do not make a decision (of loyalty –editor's addition) we have already made a decision. We <u>must</u> love/ pray for those who do not know A/Y and His Holy Living Words. We <u>must</u> be His Holy Armies. " Your People will [will be a freewill offering] volunteer freely in day of Your Power [Army]; In the splendor of Holiness] Psalm 110 :3]. We <u>must</u> be His Holy Army and His Holy witnesses [Acts 1:8] to make Him and His Holy Living Debarim/Remata known to His whole world.

A beautiful picture of the DeBar is seen in verse 105: "Your word is a lamp unto my feet and a light to my path." If ever, in the history of man on the earth; man needed a lamp unto his feet; a light to his path, it is today. American's are so lost and confused. Just look at our government today. They/we are like a ship without a sail just being blown about by the wind of every doctrine and beat about by the waves of the sea. They/we are never going to find our way as a person, as a nation, or as the world until we turn back to A/Y' Words, His will, and His way. He has created us in that way and until we cry out "not our way but <u>Your Way Yahweh</u>" [Betty's saying], we will stay confused.

"Your Word is very pure [concordance: "refined"], Therefore Your Servant loves it" (Psalm 119:140). The love of Your Word has been my guiding star, and I have had the privilege of being refined by reading and studying it for sixty-six (66) years. I have tried to fulfill Colossians 3:15-16 "Let the Peace of Christ rule [concordance: "act as arbiter"] in your heart; v 16 Let the Word of Christ richly dwell within you, with all wisdom teaching and admonishing one another [Greek says, "yourselves which must happen before we can help other"] with psalms and hymns and spiritual songs, and singing [A.T.R. in WPONT: The verb "singing" is "aido," and it is an old word for a lyrical emotion in a devout soul] with thankfulness in your hearts to God." A/Y, let us have and become drunk with Your Spirit/ Debars /Remata Words and let us stay filled with that lyrical emotion/speaking in our souls. (END) 69

Our day and night assignment is found in verses 147-148. "I rise before dawn and cry for help; I wait for your Word" What a great thing that it is to rise, to cry for help, and to wait for His Word! "My eyes anticipate the night watch that I may mediate on Your Word." How wonderful is to wait/hope in His Word, and to anticipate the night watch so that we can mediate [chew the cud Psalms 1:2b says 'And in His law he meditates [chew the cud like a cow, day and night] on Adonai/Yah Words' received that day.

The sum of the whole of Psalms 119 is found in verses 169 - 178. It says "let my cry come [near] before You O, Lord; give me understanding according to Your Word. Let my supplication come before You; deliver me according to Your Word." v172 "Let my tongue sing of Your Word, for all Your commandments [a seret hadDebar-im] are righteousness. Let Your Hand [Isaiah 63:12 Who caused His Glorious Arm to go at the right hand of Moses] be ready to help me, for I have chosen Your precepts. I long for Your salvation, O Lord, and Your Law [HadDebarim] is my delight." Let my soul be alive that I may praise You, and let your ordinances help me. I have gone astray [many times] like a lost sheep; seek your servant, for I do not forget Your commandments [HadDebarim]. O, Lord lest I/we forget.

Psalm 138:2c says, in the KJV, "For thou hast magnified thy word above all thy name." This has created great controversies about how/whether it should be translated as Word or Promise. In NASB, in the concordance, it says, "You have magnified your promise together with Your Name," and it is a definite promise to David of A/Y Faithfulness.

The only statement that I have found is in Von Rad: "That Israel knew well enough that Yahweh was the master, and not the servant, of His Words." (END) 70   A/Y is the Master of all His Words and Creation.

In Psalms 138:1 King David enlarges his thoughts about the Word: [editor] "I [David] will give You thanks with all my heart; I will sing praises to You before the gods. I will bow down toward Your Holy temple and give thanks to Your name for Your lovingkindness [hesed] and Your truth [faithfulness]. For, You have magnified Your Word [promise] according to [together with] Your name." The translation of the proposition is the key to understanding the ver. There can be no doubt that A/Y is the Master of all His Words/ His Promises/not their slave.

Psalms 138:4 says, "All the kings of the earth will give thanks to you, O Lord, [A/Y] when they have heard the Words [Debarim] of Your mouth." Oh, that this will be true. That is why A/Y needs Holy Warriors to proclaim His Holy Words before all people and the gods of the whole earth.

Psalm 150 is the summation of all the Psalms, and that is why it must be sung and memorized.

CHAPTER 11

Now, we turn **to Proverbs, Job, Song of Solomon, Ruth, Ecclesiastes, Esther, Daniel, Ezra, Nehemiah, 1 & 2 Chronicles**.

It is amazing how much the authors knew about the OT. In light of Deuteronomy 8:3d: "that He might make you understand [concordance: "know"] that man does not live by bread along, but man lives by everything [see Matthew 4:4 word] that proceeds out of the mouth of the Lord," and, Deuteronomy 30:14: "But the Word is very near you, in your mouth and in your heart, that you may observe it."

See Romans 10:8 and 2 Samuel 23:2: "The Spirit of the Lord spoke by me, and His Word was upon my tongue," and Joel 2: 28-29 [which is chapter 3:1 in the Hebrew Bible]: "I will pour out My Spirit upon all mankind [concordance: "flesh"]." It can <u>now</u> be understood how Solomon had such a deep understanding about the Spirit and the Word of A/Y in Proverbs 1:23.

Proverbs I:23 says "Turn to my reproof: 'Behold, I will pour out My Spirit upon you: I will make My Words known to you.' " A/Y says My reproof and I wonder if this is not where Paul got his statement found in 2 Timothy 3:16; 4:3: "Preach the Word; be ready in season and out of season; reprove, rebuke, exhort, with great [concordance: "all"] patience and instruction." What a challenge it is to do this with all patience [endurance/longsuffering with joy - Colossians 1:11] and instruction.

First Corinthians 14:18-19 Proclaims, "I, thank God, I speak in tongue more than you all; however, in the Church I desire to speak five words with my mind so that [in order that = a purpose clause; my commentary] I may instruct others also, rather than ten thousand words in tongue." This is not an argument against speaking in tongues, but it is written in order to instruct others in the Messianic Body so that they will not be ignorant of their own Charismata.

Also, in 1 Corinthians 14:23 it says, "Therefore, if the whole Church assembles together and all speak in tongues, and ungifted [G. Marshall idiotai 'uninstructed here in verse24 '] men or unbelievers enter, will they not say that you are mad?" This word is our word for "idiot." But it does not mean one who cannot learn, as in English, in Greek, but one who has not been instructed. So we must instruct them about the Holy Spirit as it is taught in Acts 2, 10, 19 and in 1 Corinthians 12-14.

Proverbs 1:23 proclaims: "I will pour out My Spirit upon you; I will make my words [DeBars] known to you." This confirms what I have been arguing for forty-three years and it is all through the OT. The Holy Spirit must make known the Living Words [DeBars/Ramata] of the Living A/Y to us/through us before we can see His Signs, Wonders, and Miracles being done.

This is why we must receive the Holy Spirit from [Yahve] Jesus Christ Messiah who is the Baptizer. We have the Spirit when we become born again [1 Corinthians 12: 12], but we must do as the Word says in John's gospel: 20: 21, "And when He had said this, He breathed on them and said 'Receive [Greek: LaBete Take is something they/we have to do here and in Revelation 22: 17] you the Holy Spirit."

A/Y did/does not force His Salvation upon us, nor does He force His Ruach ha Kodesh upon us. We must take both as the gift of His precious Ruach haKodesh.

Our Salvation is always unconditional because of what Jesus Christ did for us upon the Cross, but our Sanctification is always conditional depending upon our being obedient as Act 5:32 says so very clearly.

You may ask: "Why so much about the Holy Spirit here in the OT?" Because most NT believers think that the Holy Spirit is "only" a NT experience, but it is all in the OT and in the entire NT. Then, why do not most NT believers know about Him? Because they have not been instructed about Him here in America, although the Pentecostal Movement started around 1900 A.D. We must instruct them as the NT teaches.

I am going to use a personal experience that I had in 1949 related to Proverbs 3:5-7. I had preached my first sermon on September 18, and I had only been saved since August 16, so my knowledge of the Bible was very limited. I had prayed all day, September 24th, because I was to speak at a prayer meeting in the home of Bill White that night at 7:00 o'clock. I was totally blank, and I was worried that I would not have anything to say: if you can believe that.

At about 4:00 o'clock I was in Shannon, Georgia, north of Rome, when I went to the home of an American of African descent. When I knocked on her door she came to the door with a box in her hand, and she said, "Look what someone gave me at Church Sunday." She was so proud, and she was beaming with joy.

I opened it and it was a Bible.   The Book fell open to Proverbs 3:5-7. Some will say, "I don't believe that things like that happen!" But they can say what they want to; for, it did happen and I preached from that text that night, and L.C. Hampton who was going to marry Julia Ann was there and he got saved. No way can the Devil or anyone else ever make me doubt that it was the hand of A/Y that opened that Bible when I had opened the box. When we pray/ obey/He opens and our hearts burn Luke 24:32.

But, this cannot be used as an excuse for not studying the Bible and preparing oneself. It also cannot be denied that A/ Y is still opening/working and our hearts are burning. Proverbs 13:13 has a powerful word of warning. It says, "The one who despises the Word will be in [concordance: "pledged to it"] debt to it, and the one who fears the commandment will be rewarded." K & D translates it, "Whoever despiseth the word is in bonds to it, and he that feareth the commandment is rewarded." They say "Principally the Proverb has in view the Word of God as expression of the will of God."   END   71

A new understanding came to me as I read this again, because I had read John 12:47, which says, "If anyone hears My saying and does not keep them, I [Jesus Christ] do not judge him: for I did not come to judge the world, but to save the world." So, Proverbs 13:13 says, "He who despises the DeBarim /Remata is in bonds to them. But the one who fears A/Y and His Holy Debarim/Remata [Jeremiah 23:9] will be rewarded here/hereafter." This illustrates and explains both he that despises the Word 'DeBar' is bound to it, and he that fears the Commandments 'A seret hadDebarim' is rewarded because the DeBars expresses the will of A/Y better than anything that I have found up to this point. HalleluYah A/Y.

A good insight found in Proverbs 14:15, into the use of DeBar or lack of use or understanding of it, and as it is not recognized or understood by most scholars as the translation in the NASB shows, "The naive believes everything, but the sensible man considers his steps." K&D translates it: "The simple believeth every word; but the prudent takes heed to his step', and they comment "We do not translate, "everything", for "word' [DeBar] and faith are correlates, as Psalms 106:24." Yes, the De-bars/Remata and Faith are correlated in the whole OT/NT.   (END)   72

We have already discussed Psalms 106:24-25, where the DeBar is taught and understood in section 9. They despised the Land and the Word of A/Y, and they did not obey his Voice. We must obey A/Y voice and words [DeBar/Remata], for there is no other way, see Acts 5:32.

In Proverbs 15:23 we see: "A man has joy in an appropriate [concordance: "answer of his mouth"] answer, and how delightful is a timely Word [DeBar]." Here is another shade of meaning for the Word [Debar] of A/Y, for it is always a delightful and timely Word of A/Y for all those who will seek/hear and obey. Then Proverbs 25:11 provides this insight: "Like apples of gold in setting of silver is a Word spoken in right [its] circumstances." This shows that the Holy Spirit always speak the DeBar/ Remata Words at the right moment and in the Kairos of time just as the Holy Spirit spoke to me back in 3-17-13.

No one can ever look at or leave the Book of Proverbs without mentioning 31:10f. It is such a great tribute to Womanhood - to Wives and to Mothers. I read it and I give thanks to A/Y for all the Godly Women in My/Your life. WOW!

Next, we will look at **Job**: One country preacher pronounced it as "jobs." It is largely a book of philosophical speculation which is why all scholars love it, and it presents to the reader some profound questions and statements. We will look at a few of them.

First, A/Y asked Satan in 1:8: " 'Have you considered My servant Job?' For, there is no one like him on earth, a blameless and upright man, fearing God and turning away from evil. Then Satan responds in verse nine: '. . .does Job fear God for nothing?' v 10a Satan asks 'Have You not made a hedge about him and his house and all that he has, on every side?' " Yes! A/Y is our hedge on every side. This is the question that Satan and all mankind has asked since the dawn of the creation.

Job 19:25-26 has one of the most startling statements in all the OT, which is,

> "As for me, I know that my redeemer lives, and at [con. as the last] the last He will take His stand on earth , v26 Even after my skin is [con. which has been cut off] destroyed, yet from my flesh I will see God."

This is an amazing statement of faith which has been fulfilled in the OT and NT. The human heart has the ability to hope against hope. [see Romans 4:17-18]

The suffering patriarch gives to us in chapter 42:1f, the answer/summation of all questions asked by mankind? "Then Job answered the Lord and said, 'I know that You can do all things, and that no purpose of Yours can be thwarted. Who is this that hides counsel without knowledge? Therefore, I have declared that when I did not understand, things too wonderful for me, which I did not know. Hear, now, and I will speak; I will ask You, and You will instruct me [confirming 11 Tim 3:16; 4:3]. I have heard of You by the hearing of my ear; but now my eyes see You; Therefore I retract, and I repent in dust and ashes.' V7 It came about after the Lord had spoken these words [DeBars] unto Job." "I repent in dust and ashes" is the ultimate response of mankind after He/ She has seen A/Y [see Isaiah 6] by Him revealing Himself to them.

The Scrolls follow the Writing in the TLV, and now we will look at the "**Song of Solomon**" and strangely there is no use of DeBar in them.

Ruth follows, and there is not a use of DeBar in the book, but, a statement of faith and belief that is well known is given. The introduction in the NASB makes this statement: "Redemption is a key concept throughout the book; and the Hebrew Word for redemption, in its various forms, occurs twenty-three (23) times."

One of these statements is in Ruth 1:16: "But Ruth said, 'Do not urge me to leave you or turn back from following you; for where you go, I will go, and where you lodge, I will lodge. Your people shall be my people, and your God my God.' " Read the Book carefully! The conclusion of the Book in 4:21-22 gives a report of Ruth's son Obed, "And to Salmon was born Boaz, and to Boaz, Obed, v 22 and to Obed was born Jesse, and to Jesse, David." Ruth became the great, great, Grandmother Mother of King David, and she is part of Jesus Christ's lineage and heritage.

Ecclesiastes is next in the line of books to be examined. Chapter 1:1 says: "The words [DeBars] of the preacher, the son of David, the king in Jerusalem." This statement is made in the introduction of the NASB "The Septuagint [LXX] word for 'Preacher' is Ecclesiastes, from which most English titles of the book is taken". (END) 73   This quote makes a statement about [Debar] that is true for all who receive a Debar from A/Y: they all become preachers. The Debar becomes fire in their bones, as Jeremiah 20:9 points out: "But as I say, 'I will not remember Him or speak anymore in His Name, then in my heart it [the DeBar] became like a fire shut up in my bones; and I am weary of holding It in, and I cannot endure It." Preachers cannot and will not endure, and they won't "shut up" about the Holy DeBars of A/Y. Unless, like some who receive the Debar, and refuse to share it, thus deciding to shut up about His DeBars, only to see their fire go out. What a terrible place to be and a terrible thing to happen to a person. They look and act like walking dead men or women.

The fire must be kept burning. See: 2 Timothy I:6-7: "For this reason I remind you to kindle afresh the gift [charisma] of God which is in you through the laying on of my hands. For, God [A/Y] has not given us a spirit of timidity [cowardice], but the Spirit of Power, and [the Spirit] of love, and [the Spirit] of discipline[control/sound /judgment]." The reason I quoted this is because The Holy Spirit is the subject of all the above. We know that we do not have Power [Acts 1:8] within ourselves, nor love [Hased/ Agape Romans 1:5] within ourselves. Many writers translate the last word has "self-control": [self introduces the wrong subject/ noun: the Spirit is the subject]. But, the Spirit of control and of sound judgment is a much better translation and interpretation.

I was told by a dear friend that he would recommend me to a church if I would cool it about the 'charismata.' I looked at him and smiled, and I said to him, "The Bible tells me to stir it up [in the above quote], and you are telling me to cool it. Now, what am I supposed to do?" He said, "Brother Abney, I may be sinning by not recommending you to a Church." I told him that I would not take advantage of our friendship by asking him to do it. By the way, he was the first man to ask me if I was saved when I was fifteen (15) years old. So, I love him very much.

The writer of Ecclesiastes gives a statement about time in 12:1. "There is an appointed time for everything. And there is a time for every event [concordance: "delight"] under heaven—." Read all the delights. 12:10 says, "The Preacher sought to find a delightful word [DeBars] and to write words [DeBars] of truth correctly." O, that this was true of every preacher, for many don't do it because they do not know the scriptures. If done in ignorance they are forgiven, but if done because they do not study the scriptures; [2 Timothy 2:15, KJV] that is a sin, [Mark 12:24; 27 adds, 'You greatly sin'] and if we don't know the scriptures we cannot have His Holy Ruach Hakodesh/Power in/and working through us.

"The conclusion (v13), when all has been heard and it is: fear God and keep all His commandments, because this applies to every person." The preacher is to tell everyone this great/good delightful news of A/Y, and it does apply to every person.

Esther's story is one of the survival of the Jewish People, and the NASB gives this: "The setting is in Susa, the Persian capital during Ahasuerus's rule [486-465 B.C. NASB quote]."

Esther became queen, and her uncle Mordechai told her about Haman's plot to destroy all the Jews in all the entire Persian's empire.

4:1 "When Mordechai learned all that had been done; he tore his clothes, and put on sackcloth and ashes, and went out into the midst of the city and wailed loudly and bitterly." V4b Esther heard "and the Queen writhed in great anguish." This was followed by an exchange of words [debars] between Esther and Mordechai. and the most profound are in verses 13-17. Read carefully, and note verse 14: "If you remain silent at this time, relief and deliverance will arise for the Jews--and who knows whether you have not attained royalty 'for such a time as this?' " This is astounding, for the Jews are suffering the same threat to their survival today as I write this section. Who knows if this is not the time for the Gentile Church to step up for such a time as this? [See Romans 11:25]

Esther sent word to Mordecai (v 16) "Go, assemble all the Jews who are found in Susa, and fast for me; do not eat or drink for three days, night and day---and if I perish, I perish." It was none of this "fasting in the day and eating all you can through the night." Based on this request by Esther chapter 9:26 has a beautiful message "Therefore, they called these days Purim after the name of Pur. And [Therefore because of all these Words [Debars]] because of the instructions in this letter, both what they had seen in this regard/what had happened to them." This is a good example where the NASB did not record what was in the Hebrew, but put it in the concordance. It must always be translated as DeBars because the Word of A/Y has a Profound meaning in all the OT.

I do not understand why, except maybe it was what is stated by Von Rad: "On the evidence available, it could equally be argued that we see in Elijah the beginning of a concept of the Prophetic [Elijah expected Yahweh to commission him to command the rain] word which can be traced down from his own time almost to the moment when Prophecy finally disappeared."   (END)   74   I wonder what evidence Von Rad had for this statement because this great Biblical scholar was not talking about the Bible? It is clearly not the evidence in the OT or the NT.

As Paul says in 1 Thessalonians 5:16-23,   [focus on v20] do not despise Prophecies [utterance] {Greek: Marshall 'Prophecies not despise'], and later in 1 Corinthians 14:1, 5 Paul says in Greek [in order that you may keep on Prophesying].

Apparently it was from 1750, at the beginning of the scientific age that man began to question whether if there were any Prophecies or miracles or not.

This concludes our discussion of Esther.

Daniel 9:2 has a Proverbs found statement which is: "In the first year of his [Darius] reign, I, Daniel, observed in the books [was reading the Scriptures, CJB] the numbers of the years which was revealed as the word [DeBar] of the Lord to Jeremiah the Prophet for the completion of the desolations of Jerusalem, namely, seventy years."

I was happy to find that he observed in the Books or the reading the Scriptures by Daniel. This is what Paul told Timothy to do in 1 Timothy 4:13: "Until I come, give your attention [GREEK: "attendance"] [keep put your mind on] to [public not in the text] reading of Scripture, to exhortation [preaching my com], and teaching."

I did an exegetical study of the Greek in this chapter when I got out of Seminary in 1964, and it has been the guiding light/principle for my life ever since. I learned to read the Scriptures and to exercise. I wrote in the commentary which I was reading that I would read/ study the Scriptures thirty (30) Hours a week: exercise three (3) Hours a week. [4]

I have seen in my ministry so many fine young men who went to College and Seminary who did not read the Scriptures and who went out of the Ministry because they had burned out instead of being burned up by the Ruach Hakodesh of A/Y.

I heard one of my Professors say that we were going to have to learn to start studying in the Morning, and I read a statement about a man who read five (5) chapters in Genesis, Psalms, and in the NT, every day in his time of devotion. So, I started on January 1, 1965, reading this way, and I did it until 2005. I read the OT through each year and the NT through two or three times each year. I don't know who the man was, but I will when I get heaven and I will be able to thank him.

The DeBar/Rema that was hid in my heart kept me on tract until I received the baptism of the Holy Spirit in 1970. I am so thankful for A/Y Holy Spirit/DeBars/Remata words.

---

[4] I wrote in A.T. Robertson; *Word Pictures of the New Testament*, in Vol. 4,, p 580.

The seventy years in Jeremiah is quoted many times in the OT. One is 2 Chronicles 36:21 which says: "To fulfill the word [Debar] of the Lord by the mouth of Jeremiah, until the land had enjoyed its sabbaths. All the days of its desolation it kept Sabbath until the seventy years were complete." This shows how important the Sabbath was to the land and to the man for A/Y created both of them

The NT has a statement by Jesus Christ about the Sabbath which is so important. It is in Mark 2: 27: "Jesus said to them 'The Sabbath was [came into being] made for [because for the sake of] man, and not man for the Sabbath. v28 So, the Son of Man is Lord even of the Sabbath." We human beings have the Propensity to reverse things and we turn everything upside down, because sometimes we want to keep the Sabbath Holy, but we treat mankind who is most Holy as not Holy. A/Y helps us to keep man, the land, and the Sabbath all as Holy.

10:1 has an insightful statement by Daniel which says, "In the third year of Cyrus king of Persia a message [DeBar] was revealed to Daniel, who was named Belteshazzer; and the message [DeBar] was true and one of great conflict [warfare], but he understood the message [Debar] and had an understanding of the vision." An amazing thing happened here because Strong's Commentary listed it under "thing" as DeBar. K&D says: "But if Daniel had actually received a 'word' [Debar] from God, Daniel could before its fulfillment testify its truth." (END) 75

This is the best definition of the DeBar/ Rema Words of A/Y that I have found anywhere. If it is from A/Y we can testify to its truth long before it is manifested, and it is warfare [con. great conflict] when we do make it known because most people will not accept it as the true Word of A/Y until it is fulfilled.

10:6e has another statement about the man that Daniel saw which is "and the sound of his words [DeBars] like the sound of tumult [roaring]." This has the echo of Amos's word in 1:2 "He said, 'The Lord roars from Zion and from Jerusalem He utters His voice.' " Also, Isaiah 2:3f "For the law [Torah] will come forth from Zion, and the word [DeBar] of the Lord from Jerusalem," which is also based upon the words of Amos.

10:9 says "But I heard the sound of the words [DeBars]; and as soon as I heard the sounds of his words; I fell into a deep sleep on my face, with my face to the ground". This is the response of any man receiving a DeBar/Rema revelation from A/Y. He/We falls on his/our face cries out "woe is me" Isaiah 6:5.

10:11 says, "And he said to me, '0 Daniel, man of high esteem [desirability/preciousness] understand the words [Debars] that I am about to tell you and stand upright [upon your standing], for I have been now sent to you'. And when he had spoken this word to me, I stood up trembling." There it is: when A/Y' Holy Spirit speak the De-Bar/Remata words to us/ through we stand up trembling.

A personal note: When I had first received the Holy Spirit, sometimes I would stand up and I would tremble, and then Satan would say to me you are not filled with the Holy Spirit because if you were you would not be so afraid. Then I found what Paul said in 1 Corinthians 2:3: "I was with you in weakness and in fear and in much trembling." I wiped my brow, and I realized that unless I was in weakness, in fear, and much trembling I was not ready to stand up before a Holy A/Y and preach to a judgment bound people/as well as myself.

Thank be A/Y for give unto us the high and Holy opportunity to be trusted with His Holy Spirit/DeBars/Rema Word. Read 1 Tim. 1:11 -12 where Paul was telling Timothy what a great A/Y we have and what a privilege it was/is to be account worthy to be in His Service.

1 Peter 1: 14 bears witness to this services which says: "It was revealed to them [the Prophet in v10] that they were not servicing themselves, but you, in these things which now have been announced to you those who preached the Gospel to you by the Holy Spirit [The ones having Evangelized you by The Holy Spirit sent forth heaven, into which things angels long to look into." This was quoted to show how wonderful it is to be filled with the Holy Spirit and to be evangelizing in His Power. Some people want to have angel sent to them, and some people worship angels and visions, [see Colossians 2:18], but A/Y thank You for sending the Holy Spirit from heaven to Your Messianic Body and to empower it to evangelize the lost, to fulfill its ministry, [2 Timothy 3:5].

CHAPTER 12

We will take our final look at the OT by following the TLV outline and looking at **Ezra** and **Nehemiah**. A comment in the Introduction of the NASB says: "The books of Ezra and Nehemiah were one in the earliest Hebrew manuscripts, and many scholars have assumed that the author/complier of Ezra-Nehemiah was also the author of 1 & 2 Chronicles."

We will close out our look at the OT by following this order.

Ezra 1:1 says "Now in the first year of Cyrus king of Persia, in order to fulfill the word [DeBar] of the Lord by the mouth of Jeremiah, the Lord stirred up the spirit of Cyrus king of Persia so that he sent a proclamation throughout his entire kingdom."

Note Chapter 1:2-4 about the proclamation and chapter 1:5-11 about the Holy Vessels in the house of the gods of Nebuchadnezzar. We must keep all His Holy Vessels out of the houses of the gods of this world because we are His Holy Temple, [See: 1 Corinthians 3:16; 6, 19; 2 Corinthians 6:16b] "For we are the temple [naos: the Holy of Holiest] of the living God."

Paul included himself as part of this Naos with us, and we must do what 1 Corinthians 6:20 says: "For you have been bought with a price:

therefore glorify God in your body." What a challenge/a blessing this is!!!

Notice that the DeBar of the Lord, by the mouth of Jeremiah was fulfilled as all DeBars from A/Y are fulfilled. They cannot fail as Isaiah 40:8,10; 55:11 records. So much of what we say fails, but what we allow His Holy Spirit to speak in us/through us can never fail. HalleluYah: TLV in Psalms 118 uses Yah six times. Yahve is subject; Yah is the object.

There is a strong warning from Ezra in chapter 6:11 which reads: "And I [he said I not Yahve] issued a decree that any man who violates this edict [debar] a timber shall be drawn from his house and he shall be impelled on it." This shows how strong the message from Ezra was. But, it does not necessarily mean that it was A/Y who said it. Von Rad said: "We have no knowledge of any 'universalistic' opposition to the 'particularist' measures taken by Ezra and Nehemiah." (END) 76 But, we do and I know that these were difficult times, but, we have to be true to all the "DeBars of A/Y in the OT." Further, it is shown in Jonah and in Acts 20:27 "For I did not shrink from declaring to you the whole purpose [counsel, KJV] of God to You."

It clearly says in Genesis 17:5 "No longer shall your name be Abram, but your name shall be Abraham; for I [A/Y] will make you the father of a multitude of nations." It is a holy faith/belief, as Genesis 15: 6 shows, that is what A/ Y is wanting and it is a chosen race that He is making [Isaiah 53:10, 20].

This is fulfilled/clarified in 1 Peter 2:9-10, which says:

"But you are a chosen race, a royal priesthood, a Holy Nation, a people of God' possession, so that you may proclaim the excellences of Him who has called you out of darkness into His marvelous light; v 10 for you once were not A People, but now you are The People of God; you had not received mercy, but now you have received mercy."

He is the Holy A/Y of Abraham, Isaac, Jacob and the Messianic Body of Messiah with both Jews/ Gentiles that A/Y is now exalted as in all the whole OT/NT. Von Rad comments "Of course, even in the earlier narratives about prophets, the 'hero' of the story was never about the prophet himself, but rather Yahweh, who was glorified through the prophet." (END) 77

Everything that we do must be to Glorify A/Y, or we are not following the whole counsel of Him. A/Y made this unmistakable plan to Cephas in Acts 10: 34b-35 which says, "I most certainly understand now that God is not one to show partiality, but in every nation the man who fears Him and does [works righteousness] what is right is welcome to Him." What a profound revelation this was/is? James restated it again in Acts 15: 14 "Simeon has related how God first concerned Himself about taking from among the Gentiles a people for His name [see also Amos 9:11-12]," Notice A/Y concerns Himself about all people!!!!!

Ezra 10:5 has the last use of the debar by the prophet which says, "Then Ezra rose and made the leading priests, the Levites and all Israel, take oath that they would do according to this proposal [word or thing]; so they took the oath." This has to be viewed in light of the above discussion. Thanks to A/Y that man is not bound by any oath of man, but man/we are bound by the ten covenant DeBarim'--- a secret hadDeBarim of the most Holy Adonai/Yah.

John Calvin witnessed a man being burn at the stake because he did not agree with all Calvin's doctrine of predestination. Martin Luther declared in his old age that all Jews should be killed; [He may have been sick or like Solomon. Solomon's heart was turned away from God because of his foreign wives who worshiped idol gods (I Kings 11:3)], and that their Synagogue should be burned. And, Hitler responded that he was doing what Luther said and taught.

So, we must hear Paul when he said in 2 Corinthians 3:6 ". . .who also made us adequate as servants of a new covenant, not of the letter but of the Spirit; for the letter kills, but the Spirit gives life." Anything that does not give life is not of the Holy Spirit of A/Y because as John reports in 6:63: "My words [DeBar/ Remata] they are Spirit/they are Life." We must hear/do them.

Nehemiah's prayer in 1:4-11: "v4 When I heard these words [DeBars], I sat down and wept and mourned for days; and I was fasting and praying before the God of heaven. V 5 I said, "I beseech You, O Lord God of heaven, the great and awesome God, who preserves the covenant and loving-kindnesses for those who **love Him** and **keep His** commandments [HadDebarim].

Here are the conditional clauses ("for those who love Him and keep His commandments) that are found in all the promises of A/Y in the OT and the NT. There are no absolute unconditional promises in either the OT or NT. All the promises are "yes" in Messiah: 2 Corinthians 1:20, "For as many as are the promises God [A/Y in OT]; in Him [Messiah in NT] they are yes; therefore also through Him is our Amen to the glory of God through us." Our Amen is to the Glory of A/Y in/ through us.

Read all the book from Chapter 2 through 8:10, which says: "Then Nehemiah, who was the governor [Tirshatha a Persian title], and Ezra the priest and scribe [this is why some say Ezra wrote Ezra, Nehemiah, and 1&2 Chronicles] and the Levites [who taught the people] said to all the people 'This day is Holy to the Lord your God [A/Y]; do not mourn or weep.' For, all the people were weeping when they heard the Words of the law. V10 Then he said to them, 'Go, eat of the fat, drink of the sweet, and send portions to him who has nothing prepared; for this day is Holy to our Lord [A/Y]. Do not be grieved, for the Joy of the A/Y is your strength.' " Some said that "A/Y's strength is in our Joy." His Holy Spirit is both our Strength Acts 1:8 and Joy 13:52. The Book of Nehemiah concludes with this statement in 8:12: "Because they understood the words [Debars] which had been made known to them."

This is the purpose of the fivefold ministries in Ephesians 4:11-12a: "He [A/Y/Messiah] gave some as apostles, and some as prophets, and some as evangelists, and some as pastors and teachers; For the equipping [Greek "perfecting"; and most will not translate this correctly because it says perfecting, but that is what it is here and in 2 Corinthians 13:11] of the saints for [into/ unto] the work of service, to [into/unto] the building up of the body of Christ [Messiah]." I have never known anyone, whether a pastor or layman who was not trying to perfect himself/herself to do any work of ministering or the building up of the body of Christ [Messiah]. It just does not happen.

1 Chronicles repeats most of what is in 1&2 Kings, and Samuel. A statement in the Introduction says: "The Septuagint [The Greek

translation of the O.T. or LXX] translators dubbed the book 'the things omitted,' indicating that they regarded it as a supplement to Samuel/Kings." This will help us understand the two books.

1 Chronicles 10:13-14 has a summary of Chapters 1-9 which says: "So Saul died for his trespass which he committed against the Lord [A/Y], because of the word [DeBars] of the Lord which he did not keep ; and also because he asked counsel of a medium making inquiry of it, v14 and did not inquire of the Lord. Therefore He killed him and turned the kingdom over to David the son of Jesse." They/We are demanded to make inquiry of A/Y, and there are some theological problems about whether the Lord killed him or that he killed himself by not keeping the DeBars of A/Y. We will make this point clear in the NT. It is discussed in Romans 9:22.

Chapter 16:15 gives an important statement about the Covenant and the DeBars, which is: "Remember His Covenant forever, the word [Debars] which He commanded to a thousand generations." We would say to keep His Covenant and DeBars to all generations because they are His and they are Eternal/Absolute. Wow! Here is that word and many will not accept this as a moral absolute. But here it is!

Chapter 25:5-6;16 has a new insight into the meaning of Debar that says, "All these were sons of Heman the king's seer [TLV in matters pertaining to God, were there to exult God]] to exult him according to the words [DeBars], v 16 and all these were under the direction of their father to sing in the house of the Lord." The singing of the DeBars' unto A/Y in His House is to be continuously singing Praise to exult A/Y.

2 Chronicles 6:10,17 reveals: v10 says "Now the Lord has fulfilled His word which He Spoke; for I have risen in the place of my Father David,

as the Lord promised [spoke]." A/Y always fulfills His Word [DeBar] which He Spoke, and He always will! HallaluYah! Verse 17 records: "Now therefore, O Lord, the God of Israel, let Your Word be confirmed which You have spoken to Your Servant David." A/Y always <u>fulfills</u> and <u>confirms</u> His DeBars, De-Barim, and a seret HadDaberim

Chapter 18:4 fulfills and confirms all the above statement, "Moreover, Jehoshaphat said to the king of Israel, 'Please inquire first [at this time] for a word of the Lord.' " We must at all times inquire at this <u>"time"</u> for the Word from A/Y. This will keep us from assuming that the Word of yesterday/day is sufficient for today. Now, I understand what Jesus Christ said in Matthew 6:34, "Do not worry about tomorrow; for tomorrow will care [worry about itself] for itself, [according to Commentary in NASB: "Sufficient for the day is its evils."] This proves how we can understand the NT only when we know what the OT teaches. The reason there is so much misunderstanding of the NT is because we do not <u>read</u>/<u>study</u> the OT.

Verses 12-13 of Chapter 18 further clarifies the above. "Then the messengers who went to summon Micaiah spoke to him saying, 'Behold, the words of the Prophets are uniformly favorable to the kings. So please let your word be like one of them and speak favorably.' v 13 But, Micaiah said, 'As the Lord lives, what my God says, that I will speak.' "

This confirms what Numbers 22: 18, 20, 36 says, regarding Balaam's words to Balak's messengers. This is amazing how Balaam told them in 18c "I could not do anything, either small or great, contrary to the command [mouth/De-bars] of the Lord my God." He said "the Lord My God," and this is what we must understand that we cannot do anything either small or great without the Power of A/Y working in/ through us as Acts 1:8 says.

2 Chronicles 18:23-24, shows what happens to the true prophet when false prophets do not agree: "Then, Zedekiah the son of Chenaanah came near/struck Micaiah on the cheek and said, 'How [which way] did the Spirit of the Lord pass from me to speak to you, 24 Micaiah said, 'Behold, you will see on the day when you enter an inner room to hide yourself.' " Listen to the arrogance in the question that Zedekiah asked Micaiah: "How [which way] did the Spirit of the Lord pass from me to speak to You?" He thought that he had control of the Spirit of the A/Y as many people do today, but we can never have control of the Spirit of A/Y, for He must have control over us, Isaiah 42:1; 1 Corinthians 12:11, "But one and the same Spirit works all these things, distributing to each one individually just as He wills." There is one and only one and the same Spirit of A/Y, and He manifests/distributes to each one individually as He wills. This is the working of the Spirit of A/ Y on individual, and it is always A/Y Wills/Spirit and not man.

Chapter 34:16- 19 reiterates: "Then Shaphan [the scribe] brought the book to the king and reported further word [DeBar] to the king, v19 When the king heard the words of the law, he tore his clothes." He tore his clothes as a sign of conviction, and he repented in sack cloths and ashes.

Moving on through the chapter we find in verse 22-27: Huldah the prophetess spoke in v26 "Thus says the Lord God of Israel regarding the words [DeBars] which you have heard, v27 "Because your heart was tender and you humbled yourself before the God when you heard His words against this place and its inhabitants." We must hear His Words

127

and humble ourselves before Him in sack clothes and ashes before He can perform signs, wonders, and miracles in/through us. A/Y helps us to humble ourselves and repent for our personal sins and the sins of our nation.

Remember that we have only to look at the Debars/Ramata that give us some new understanding and meaning of these great Debars/Remata so that we can <u>know</u> and <u>do</u> them.

We will <u>now</u> turn to the NT.

CHAPTER 13

The New Covenant

A <u>New</u> <u>Covenant</u> was promised by A/Y to Israel and the nations of the world through Jeremiah. In Jeremiah 31: 31-33, Jeremiah writes: " 'Behold, the days are coming,' declares the Lord, 'when I will make a New Covenant with the house of Israel and with the house of Judah.' v33 'But this is the covenant which I will make with the house of Israel after those days,' declares the Lord, 'I will put My Law [a seret had Debarim' the Living Words of the Living A/Y'] within them and on their hearts I will write it; and I will be their God, and they shall be My People.' "

Not only did Jeremiah know how circumcision was required for an Israelite to be accepted by A/Y as noted in Jeremiah 4:4c: "Circumcise yourselves to the Lord and remove the foreskins of your heart, men of Judah and the inhabitants of Jerusalem, or else the wrath will come like a fire." He also knew that there had to be a New Covenant written on their heart if they were going to be His People and He was going to be their A/Y. So, we turn to the New Covenant to see this fulfilled. We discuss it at 1 Corinthians 11:25.

We must look at the comparison or relationship between **DeBar** in the OT and **Rema** in the NT. The only two places that I have found them being mentioned together are in A.T. Robertson: "Literally, sayings [Remata Words, lit. Greek], but like the Hebrew dabhar for 'word' it is used here for 'things.' "   (END)   78

And, in *The Expositor's Greek New Testament:* "In Paul's Epistles and in Hebrews, it [Rema] appears to be used mostly, if not exclusively, of a word proceeding directly or indirectly from God. It has indeed another sense, that of 'things' corresponding to the Hebrew, DeBar, 'the thing spoken of' 'the thing enjoined' [i.e. Matthew 23: 16; Luke 1:37, 2:17; Acts 10: 37; 2 Corinthians 13:1]." Both are used of Words spoken directly from Adonai/ Yah or indirectly by the prophets who A/Y has appointed, anointed, commissioned/ commanded by His Holy Spirit under shadow of His Hand to speak His Words in/through us. HalleluYah to our A/Y. (END)   79

This above tell us about the New Covenant that A/Y will make with the house of Israel and the house of Judah, and in v 33 it is with Israel, and it is fulfilled in the NT as it is revealed in the first twelve chapters.

Matthew 4:4 and **Luke** 4:4 have the first use of the Rema Word in the NT based on Deuteronomy 8:3 which is: "It is written, Man shall not live on bread along, but by every Word [Rema] that proceeds out of the Mouth of God." A/Y/Messiah's DeBars/Rema(s) are Spirit and they are life [John 6:63]. It is true that mankind who does not live on His Rema just exist/not live.

Remember now that we are only looking at words that give a new meaning to Remata. Matthew 18:16b says: ". . .so that [in order that: it is a purpose clause] by the mouth of two or three witnesses every fact [Rema Word] may be confirmed." This is what Jesus Christ taught, and it is where Paul got what he taught in 1 Thessalonians 5: 20-21 which says: "Greek "prophecies" not despices, v 21 but prove all things, the good hold fast"; 1 Corinthians 12:10; 14:29 says, "Prophets two or three let them speak, and the others let discern."

All Remata Words of A/Y must be discerned/confirmed by the Messianic Body as it is at Worship. None of this "Lone Ranger" stuff where one can claim that he is speaking the truth because Messiah lives inside of him/ her. This is the apex of hubers/ arrogances, and it contradicts what the OT and NT says in 1 Corinthians 14:16f. It is to Err, and to greatly error. Mark 12:24, 17.

Matthew 26:75 records a statement we need to hear because it tells us that Peter remembered "And Peter remembered the word {Rema} which Jesus had said, 'Before a rooster crows, you will deny Me three times.' And he went out and wept bitterly." What a revealing comment given in Matthew about Peter; and it tells about his reaction to remember what Rema Jesus Christ' had said/spoken. When we remember how many times Jesus Christ/A/Y/ has spoken His Divine [DeBar/Rema] Word to us we to must bow down and weep bitterly. He speaks, we weep, and we Worship.

Now we will look at the Gospel of **Mark**. It is surprising that Rema is used only in chapters 9:32; and 14:72. In 9:1 it says: "And Jesus was saying to them, 'Truly I say unto you, there are some of those standing here who will not taste death until they see the Kingdom of God after it has come in Power" [see Acts 1:8], and, Matthew 16:28 has this same quote. The word to be emphasized here is after the Kingdom of God has come in Power on the day of Pentecost. The Kingdom of Jesus Christ has come in Power now: HalleluYah be to Adonai/Yah.

Mark 9:32 gives an insight into how the Disciples felt when they did not understand Jesus Christ's Words. "But they did not understand {were not knowing} this statement [Greek says: 'But they did not know the Rema, and feared Him to question']." This shows how scholars struggle to translate the DeBar in the FC and the Rema in the NC, and they say "this statement not Rema."

Many scholars say that Matthew 3:11 and Luke 3:15 got it all wrong, when they said: "They would be baptized in the Holy Spirit and Fire," but Mark records this as the understanding that Peter had from his life as a fisherman.

Mark 9:49 says "Everyone will be salted with Fire." Salt both preserves meat and flavors it. The Holy Spirit's Fire preserves and flavors the life of believers when we have been baptized by the Holy Spirit; or we have received the Anointing from the Holy One/Messiah; as it says in 1 John 2;20, 27.

In 1 John 1:20 the KJV says "But ye have an unction from the Hole One, and ye know all things." There are two things wrong with this translation, and they are: First, the word "unction" is an old English word meaning "anointing." Why did they use unction instead of anointing which they clearly used in verse 27? Because, the translators would have had to ask themselves if they had ever received the anointing from the Holy One? So, it was easier for them to use unction

than anointing, but in verse 27 they used the correct word –
"anointing." See it there, and memorize it.

The other mistranslation is in "you will know all things." This is a
misunderstanding between the word "panta" which is used in Greek as
a philological term to mean "all things" and "pantes" which is used
here. It means you will <u>know</u> it.   One man who I was sharing with over
the phone told me that someone told him that he had the Holy Spirit
but did not know it. The Holy Spirit gave me the answer like a flash of
lighting; I told him that I had believed that same thing for twenty-one
(21) years, but if you have something and do not know it; you could
lose it and not know it. Not so with the Holy Spirit, because I John 2:27
[Greek: <u>commands</u>] "<u>abide</u> <u>in</u> <u>Him</u>."

The other use is in Mark 14:72 which repeats the Words of Jesus Christ
given to Peter in Mark 9:32.

<u>Now,</u> we come to **Luke,** authored by the beloved Greek Physician who
was also a great Greek Historian. A.T. Robertson points out: "This
scientific physician comes to the study of the life of Christ with a
trained intellect, with an historian's method of research, with a
physician's care in diagnosis and discrimination, and with reverence for
and loyalty to Jesus Christ as Lord and Saviour." END 80   The
importance of Luke cannot be overestimated, and Robertson says, "He
is the first critic of the sources of the Gospels and a scholarly one."
(END) 81   Because of Luke and Paul, the Gospels survived the critical
acid test of the eighteenth century scholars who questioned the
truth/validity of the documents of the whole OT and NT in the Bible.

Where Luke came from, and how he became involved with Paul we do not know, but we must be eternally grateful to A/Y for him. Because we would be utterly lost about the early History of the Messianic body of Jesus Christ and Paul' mission trips if the Holy Spirit had not revealed/wrote Acts by Dr. Luke.

Now, we will look at Luke's amazing book. In Chapter 1:35-37, Luke repeats two OT statements: one is found in Isaiah 7:14 which says: "The angel answered and said to her [Mary], 'The Holy Spirit will come upon you, and the power of the Most High will overshadow you; and for that reason the Holy Child shall be called the son of God. v37 For nothing [not any Word] will be impossible with God [as Genesis 18:14]."

In 2 Corinthians 12:9 we find a connection: "And He said unto me, 'My grace is sufficient for you, for My [Greek: "the [My] the article is used as a pronoun"] power is perfected in weakness.' Most gladly, therefore, I will rather boast about [not about which many do but in] my weaknesses, so that [in order that] the Power of Christ may dwell [overshadow me, same word in Luke 1:35] in me." I don't know about you, but this shouting ground for me. That this same Power that overshadowed Mary and created in her womb the Messiah, overshadows/creates /reveals in us His Rema Word.

Similarly, Luke 1:37 says what is found in Genesis 18:14: "Is there anything too difficult [Wonderful] for the Lord?" A.T. Robertson states: "Rhema brings out the single item rather than the whole content [Logos the whole Gospel]."   (END) 82   No, there is nothing to difficult/wonderful for Adonia/Yah our Living Abba heavenly Father [See Ephesians 3:20f].

We can't miss or pass by verse 38 without hearing Mary's answers: "And Mary said 'Behold, the bond slave [Greek: "doulee"] of the Lord; may it be done to me according to your word [Rema]." We must do and say the same thing when the Messiah speaks through the Holy Spirit a word [Debar/Rema] unto us/through us: "be it according to Thy word."

Luke 1:65 gives an astounding response from the people after John was born "Fear came upon all those living around them; and all the matters [Rema] were being talked about in all the hill country of Judea." This will happen in all the hills around Macon and any town when people see this miraculous work in the Body of Messiah.

The birth of Jesus Christ is recorded in Chapter 2 of Luke's Gospel. There are nine "Remata" used in chapter 1 & 2; and there is a reason for that: A.T. Robertson says, "To the end of chapter 2 we have the most Hebraistic [Aramaic] passage in Luke's writings, due evidently to the use of documents or notes of oral tradition." (END) 83 So, Luke knew about the use of [DeBars] in the OT, and also Luke knew and quoted from the LXX [Seventy] which was the translation of the Hebrew Bible into Greek in about 200 B.C. And, Luke knew all about oral tradition that some want to put it above the Holy Writ today.

Luke 2:14-15 must be quoted: "Glory to God in the highest, and on earth peace among men with [of good pleasure/will] whom He is pleased; v15 when the angels had gone away from them into heaven, the shepherds began saying to one another. 'Let us go straight to Bethlehem then, and see this thing [Rema] that has happened which the Lord has make known unto us.' " These DeBar/ Rema Word/ Events always happen if they are made known unto us by the Holy Spirit/from A/Y. What a great A/Y we have, and we [dei/must] wait/serve.

Next we look at Chapter 1:51 says, "He went down with them and came to Nazareth, and He continued in subjection to them, and His mother treasured all these sayings [Remata] in her heart." We, too, must treasure all A/Y DeBarim/ Remata Words in our heart, for they will be like a "burning fire in our bones, see Jeremiah 20:9b."

Luke 3:2f reports: "In the high priesthood of Annas and Caiaphas, the Word [Rema] of God came to [Greek says: **upon**/**remained**: they remain when the Holy Spirit writes them on our hearts 2 Corinthians 3:3] John, the son of Zacharias, in the wilderness, and he came into the district around the Jordan, preaching a baptism of repentance for the forgiveness of sins." This shows what John was preaching and therefore, how we must listen and do what they did and repent!!!!

There is a clear and wonderful contrast between the Logos [Gospel] which tells about what /where Jesus Christ was preaching, and the use of the Rema [single Word spoken]Word which tells what the Logos does in Chapter 5:1.

A/Y never uses anything that "belongs" to us without blessing us for it. Jesus Christ told Simon what to do for his blessing, and "Simon answered and said, 'Master, we have worked hard all night and caught nothing, but I will do as You say [at your Rema], and let down the nets." [Luke 5:5] This not only explains the Logos as teaching, but it also shows that Jesus Christ gave Simon a Rema Word just like He does us, and we must do what Simon did and say what he said: "nevertheless, at Your Rema Word I will let down the nets." Let us let down the evangelism nets/catch men. We will catch men as it says in 5:10c, "And Jesus said unto Simon, 'Do not fear, from now on you will be catching men.' " This gives us a wonderful opportunity to study a Greek word in 5:10.

The word is used only two places in the NT here and in 2 Timothy 2:26. It says here in the Greek: "Fear thou not; from now on thou will be taking men alive." It was in 1975, when I first studied/saw this word, and I was asked by my pastor, Robert Akins, who baptized Ruby and me, to preach a Revival in Thomaston, Georgia. He was telling me about preaching on this scripture, and how that the Lord revealed to him that "when you caught a fish you catch it from <u>life</u> to <u>death</u>, and when you catch a man/woman /child you catch them from <u>death</u> to <u>life</u>." HalleluYah: Let us fish!

I told him that A/Y had revealed to him the meaning of the Greek word Zogreo. A.T. Robertson says about this word: "Zogreo means to catch alive, not to kill." What a joy/ delight it is to be used by Jesus Christ Messiah to catch men/women /and children alive! [See. 1 Peter 1:12] (END) 84 "through the [ones] having been evangelized by the Holy Spirit." Maybe this is why we don't see more evangelizing because we don't do it through the H. S.

And now, I have been setting you up for the other use of Zegreo in 2 Timothy 2:26, which is in Greek: "And they may turn out of the snare of the devil, having been caught by him [,] to the will of that one." In the footnote of the Greek translation it says "That is, God" [the remoter antecedent]. [5]

This tells the story how and why translators will not translate the Greek as Paul used it correctly. It does not refer to the remoter antecedent which is God, but it refers to the Devil who can/does take us alive if we give him a place in our lives. A beautiful discussion of this is in Ephesians 4:25-32; read it!

Ephesians 4:26f says: "And do not give the devil an opportunity [lit a place]." When he has what we call a small place in our lives he can take us alive any time he wills/wishes, and we are dead to the Will/Work of A/Y. This blows the mind of most modern day scholars/believers because they/we do not take our little/small sin seriously enough. Some modern day Preachers do not say sin anymore, they use the word "mistakes" which is usually not our fault, but it is our parents, culture, or better yet "that other man or woman," not us who "made us" sin.

In Exodus 20:20, the vision is perfectly clear [2020 vision]. A/Y says/gives through Moses the answer: "Moses said to the people, 'Do not be afraid; for God had come in order to test you, and in order that the fear of Him may remain [be before] with you, so that you may not sin.' " How much plainer can A/Y make it – that sin separates us from Him? And, sins destroy our bodies which are His Holy Naos [Holy of Holiest] Temples?

---

[5] [The remoter antecedent refers back to God in verse 25 rather than to the Devil taking him captive to the will of that one.]

Just in case you think that this is just in the OT let me repeat from the NT for you/us what Paul said in Romans 7:13. I just have to quote the Greek here because it is so clear. "Therefore, the good to me became death? May it not be; yet sin, in order that it might appear sin, through the good working death to me, in order that sin through the commandment [a seret hadDeBarim] might become excessively sinful." When sin becomes exceedingly sinful to us as individuals/Churches and our nation then 2 Chronicles 7:14 will become a reality in our life and the life of our nation. Sin is only taking that which is good and making evil out of it. Everything that A/Y created is very good. Satan and man takes good and makes it sin which is very bad.

We must quote Ephesians 4:30 here because sin in the life of a believer does what this verse says. Here it is: "Do not grieve the Holy Spirit of God, by [Greek is "very clear"] whom you were sealed for the day of redemption." This is based on Isaiah 63:10 which says, "But they rebelled and grieved His Holy Spirit; therefore He turned Himself to become their enemy, He fought against them." There are two wrestling matches which we cannot win, like Jacob in Genesis 32:24f, and this one. IF we surrender to A/ Y, sins cannot control our lives.

Romans 6:17-18 gives us a sidebar that proves the above statement. It says: "But thanks be to God that [con you were slaves…but you became] became obedient from the heart. A. T. Robertson: "to that form of teaching ye were delivered." This translation is not made clear in most translation, but verse 18 explains it as: "and having been freed from sin you became slaves of righteousness." Here it is made very clear either we are alive to A/Y or to the Devil. We must choose which one. See Deuteronomy 30: 19-20 and choose.

Another way the word "Remata" is translated in the NT is found in chapter 7:1 which says: "When He [Jesus Christ] had completed all His discourse [Remata] in the hearing of the people He went to Capernaum." This verse shows how many ways the word Remata is translated in the NT. It <u>must</u> always be translated as Rema and not things/discourse.

 Also, Chapter 9:45 gives a double use of the word Rema: "But they did not understand this statement [Rema], and it was concealed from them so that they would not perceive it; and they were afraid to ask Him about the statement [Rematous]." Rema is translated as discourse above statement here, and this may be the first time that Jesus Christ told His disciple about His death and it was concealed; they did not understand it, and they were afraid to ask Him about it. Thanks be unto A/Y that we have the Holy Spirit as our teacher [John 14:26; I John 2:27] who will teach/ guide us in all that we need to know and to do as He speaks the Remata in us.

The above passage is made clear (regarding their "understanding) in Chapter 18:34 since in the Greek it says: "And they none of these things understood, and this Rema was having been hidden from them, and they knew not the things being said." This does not mean that A/Y hides His Ways/Will from us because His whole creation and His revelation is not to hide but to reveal. There are no hidden vision/illusion that someone has to reveal to us in secret. They are all revealed in Messiah who is the true mystery according to Colossians 2:2.

The Greek in Chapter 2:2 says: "In order that the heart of them may be comforted, being joined together in love, and for all riches of the full assurance of understanding, for full knowledge of the mystery of God, Christ." Here it is: the full assurance and the full knowledge of the mystery of God: Messiah. There is no more or none other.

The rest of Luke continues in Chapter 14.

CHAPTER 14

I call this <u>the answer</u> that answered all of mankind's questions: <u>Messiah.</u>

He is the ANSWER!

We see a picture of the Messiah's persona changing wisdom in Luke 20:26. It reveals the ulterior motive of those who are trying to trap Jesus Christ by questioning Him. But, ". . . they unable to catch ['catch His statement'] Him in a saying {Rema} in the presence of the peoples; and being amazed at His answer, they became silent." We must sometime be silenced/hushed in His Presence.

Jesus Christ answered all the questions about His Life in Mark 12: 35-37, which is based on Psalms 110:13. What a profound revelation of the scriptures is revealed in Jesus Christ's answer based on His understanding of His Life and His Work. In Matthew 22:46, it says, "No one was able to answer Him a word, nor did anyone dare from that time on to ask Him another [any longer] question." I call this <u>the answer</u> that answered all of mankind's questions: <u>Messiah.</u> He is the ANSWER /He does this if we allow Him!!!

In Chapter 24:8, 11, there is a strange thing that happens. None of the sources that I have discuss verse eight (8). I think it may be because it has the word Rema in both of the above previous verses, for these accounts by Luke show how distorted/disturbed His disciples were as sometime we are. In verse eight (8) which says, "And they remembered His Words" the scholars had to translate the Remata Word correctly because it doesn't make sense to translate it as thing. Further, verse 11 helps us with the rejection by those who Heard Jesus Christ's words: "But these Words [Remata] appeared to [in their sight] them as nonsense, and they would not believe them." This is the way the DeBar/Rema Words appears to all the people who do not know A/Y, but we [who are known by Him Gal 4:9a] know them to be true.

Paul says in 1 Corinthians 2:14: "But a natural [an unspiritual] man does not accept the things of the Spirit of God, for they are foolishness to him; and he cannot understand them, because they are spiritual appraised [examined]." So, do not expect the carnal believer [1 Corinthians 3:14], or the worldly man or woman to understand the DeBars/Remata preached to him/her: they are only for born from above [John 3:3] and Holy Spirit driven people. [Romans 8:16]

These were Jesus Christ's disciples who did not believe His Remata Words until after the day of Pentecost, and this is why each believer must receive the Holy Spirit for himself or herself. The Rema Words just does not make sense to the natural man or woman now any more than it did to His early Disciples. We now turn to Acts: Luke's second Book.

In Acts 2:14, Cephas [Paul always used Cephas] preached his first sermon which says, "And, Peter, taking [being put forward as spokesman] his stand with the eleven, raised his voice and declared to them: men of Judea and all you who live in Jerusalem, let this be known to you and give heed to my words [Remata]." He raised his voice [I'm glad he raised his voice] and declared his word as Remata. All preaching should be declaring as 2 Timothy 4:2 says: "Preach the Word [Logos which is the whole Gospel]" of which the Rema is the specific item of A/Y. This is why we must preach expository sermons in order that the people will know that it is the DeBar/Rema Words of A/Y and not just our opinion or some other man's opinion.

Acts 5:20 has a beautiful statement about what we are to do when we have been released from all our past sin and failure. We are to "Go, stand and speak [continue to speak] to the people in the temple the whole messages [all the Remata] of this Life." This is what the DeBars [Deuteronomy 20:1920]/Rema Words are: they are the Words of this Life as in John 14:6.

Now, we come to one of the most important uses of the Rema in 5:27-32 in the NT. The whole text must be used or verse 32 will not be understood.

> ²⁷ *When they had brought them, they placed them before the Sanhedrin. The kohen gadol questioned them,* ²⁸ *saying, "We gave you strict orders not to teach in this name—and look, you have filled Jerusalem with your teaching, and you intend to bring on us the blood of this Man!"*

> ²⁹ *Peter and the emissaries replied, "We must obey God rather than men.* ³⁰ *The God of our fathers raised up Yeshua, whom you seized and had crucified.* [a] ³¹ *This One God exalted at His right hand as Leader and Savior,* [b] *to give repentance to Israel and removal of sins.* ³² *And we are witnesses of these events—as is the Ruach ha-Kodesh, whom God has given to those who obey Him."*

I had repeated Acts 5:32 for forty-three (43) years, and I had never asked what these things in the KJV were? When I received this new insight on the meaning of the text it blew my mind.

As you reread the whole section and look closely at verses 29-31, which says in Greek: "And answering Peter and the Apostles and said; It behooves us [must] to obey God rather than man, v30 The God of the Fathers of us raised Jesus, whom ye killed hanging on a tree; v31 this man God a Ruler and a Saviour exalted to the right hand of Him to give repentance to Israel and the forgiveness of sins." [The Greek has this one right – 'that He might give repentance and the forgiveness of sins to Israel.] This is what A/Y revealed to me that He had exalted Jesus Christ that He might give repentance and forgiveness of sins to Israel. WOW!

How could anybody ever preach or teach "replacement theology" when A/Y had provided repentance and forgiveness of Sins to Israel and us in Jesus Christ?

 If we look at Romans 8:4, which revelation I received just a few days ago, then we will see clearly what Paul says about the Law/Torah. It says according to A.T. Robertson, "The ordinance of the Law [to dikaioma tou nomou] The requirement of the Law ." [In order] that they be fulfilled in us who walk not in the flesh, but in the Spirit." They did not end. They were/are fulfilled in us when we walk in the Spirit. (END) 85

Now, v 32 makes perfect good sense to me and I hope to you "And we are witnesses to these things [remata]; and so is the Holy Spirit whom God has given to them that obey Him." There are two things that must be understood about this verse:

A. That A/Y has provided repentance and the forgiveness of sins unto Israel and to us. If He had not provided repentance and forgiveness of sins to Israel how could we know that He has provided repentance and forgiveness to us as 11:18 shows. We would not know: but because He has; we know it and now we can receive the message of verse 31.

B. The other is that we must know that A/Y can only give His Holy Spirit to those who obey Him. If He could give us His Holy Spirit while we were disobeyed then He could have forgiven us our sins without our Messiah having to die upon the cross/ tree. Thanks be to A/Y for coming in Messiah and for reconciling us to Himself on the cross.

The first problem that arose in the early Jewish Messianic Body of Messiah is introduced in chapter 6:1ff, and it gives us the way all problems are to be handled in His Body. Men were chosen that were filled with and led by the Holy Spirit. Listen what was said about Stephen in verse 5b: "And they chose Stephen a man full of faith and the Holy Spirit, and Phillip." It did not say that Phillip was full of the Holy Spirit, and the first time I told some one about this they said "No, you are wrong." So, I had to find someone who had translated this passage correctly.

A.T. Robertson says "Nothing is here told of any of the seven except Stephens who is 'a man full of faith and the Holy Spirit', and Nicolas 'a proselyte of Antioch'", and we don't hear any more about Nicolas.

(END)   86

But Phillip had to have the Apostle from Jerusalem to come down to Samaria to lay hand on them to receive the Holy Spirit, and this is why I said that he did not have the Spirit until after he baptized the Ethiopian' eunuch: he was caught away by the Holy Spirit. [see 8:39b] A wonderful conclusion to Phillip's life is given in 21:89, which says:

> "On the next day we left and came to Caesarea, and entering the house of Phillip the evangelist, who was one of the seven, we stayed with him.   v9 Now this man had four virgin daughters who were prophetesses."

What a testimony for Phillip to have four virgin daughters and to have Paul, Silas, Timothy, and Luke in his home as the result of his being caught away by the Spirit.

It would have been great to hear the conversation of that group, and it is **essential** that we also be caught/[possessed by in 10:44 epepesen/epipipto to take possession as in 8:16, by Dale Moody] away by the Holy Spirit and to walk in Him as Paul said in Galatians 5:22. How would you like to have entertained that group?   (END)   87

The conclusion of book 1 in Acts is given in 6:7. There are five more. Two are in 9:31; 12:24 about Peter and the Jewish Jerusalem Messianic Body of Jesus Christ. The last three are about Paul and the Body at Antioch which are 16:6; and 19:21; 28:30. These are dated by beginning at 30 A.D. and are repeated every five years, and they are very important for us to know the History of the Messianic Body of Jesus Christ/Paul's mission trips to the Gentiles.

In Chapter 6:8, we see what happens to a man or woman when they are full of faith and the Holy Spirit which says: "And, Stephen, full of grace and power, was performing great wonders and signs [attesting miracles] among the people." If these great wonders/signs attesting miracles are not being performed among the people by us then there is a question of whether or not we are full of faith, grace, Power of the Holy Spirit. Help us to be continuously <u>full</u> of the Holy Spirit so that You can <u>perform</u> Your Miracles, so that He can perform His ministry.

See/Read, chapter 7 for Stephen's great sermon that baffles all great Scholars and us.

The Messianic Body of Jesus Christ is catapulted and <u>expanded</u> out of the Jewish World into the Gentile World, according to chapter 10:17. Read carefully about Cornelius's vision, a Roman who may have help established the Roman Church, and no reference is made to him by any scholars about Cephas's visions preached to Cornelius. Verse 22 tells about what the group from Cornelius said: "And they said, Cornelius, a centurion, a righteous and a God fearing man well-spoken of by the entire nation of the Jews, was divinely directed by a holy angel to send for you to come to his house and [to]hear a message [remata Words] from you." Here the translator says "message" and in v44 "discourse," but most places they say "things."

In v 44 it says in the Greek "While Peter was still speaking these words [Remata] the Holy Spirit fell on all the ones hearing the discourse 'logon.' " This shows the correct way to translate both the Rema Word and the Logos Word. The Rema is when the Holy Spirit speaks it into our heart and it becomes the Living Word of the Living A/Y to us. Then we listen/learn the Logos discourse/message!!

I have been praying for a scriptural clarification of these two Words for many years, **and now here they are fully explained. I knew in my heart that this was/ is the way they must be translated at most places. Thanks A/Y.**

Further light is shed on the events of Chapter 10, by the passage in 11:14-18 – when v14 says: "And he [Cephas] will speak words to you by which you will be saved, you and all your whole household." This shows what must happen before one can be saved. He/She must be hearing the DeBars/Re mata Words spoken through messengers by the Holy Spirit. A doctrine of household salvation is based upon this verse which is true if everyone in the household believes. Romans 10:13 says, "For whosoever calls upon the Name of the Lord will be saved." It is that clear! HalleluYah!

See how "the words of life are used in the following:

> *v15 "And as I began to speak, the Holy Spirit fell on them just as He did on us at the beginning.*

> *v16 "And I remembered the word [remata words it should say] of the Lord, how He used to say, 'John baptized with water, but you will be baptized with [in] the Holy Spirit."* [I love that word in the Holy Spirit and not just with, see John 14:17.]

v17 "Therefore if God gave to them the same gift as He gave us also after believing in the Lord Jesus Christ, who was I that I could stand [prevent God] in God's way?

v18 "When they heard this, they quieted [they became silent] and glorified God, saying, 'Well then , God has <u>granted</u> to the Gentiles also the repentance that leads to life'". [Indeed, the same thing that is said about the Jews in 5:31, AY <u>gave</u>, is said about the Gentile here He <u>granted</u> 10:18]

A/Y did/does <u>give</u> in 5:31/ and here He <u>grants</u> unto all the gift of repentance that leads to life [Betty had said to me many times that **repentance is a gift**]. This is so important because it is rehearsed in Chapter 15, and it opens the door of Salvation **to** all who <u>believed</u> on A/Y, see Romans 10:13 and **to** all who <u>call</u>.

The thought is continued in 13:42 it says: "As Paul and Barnabas were going out, the people kept begging that these things [Remata] might be spoken to them the next Sabbath." People are still begging today for the DeBars/Remata to be spoken unto them <u>now</u>. Some do not even know that it is the DeBars/Remata Words of the Living A/Y that they want or that they need. They are the Words of Life [John 6:63] that they must have, to possess eternal life now.

One of the most important dates in the NT is given in 18:11; because, Claudius in 49 A.D drove all the Jews out of Rome, and Shaul met Aquila and Priscilla in Corinth and worked with them for some time making tents. Here we receive an important bit of information that changed Paul's life and the life of the Messianic body forever. He wrote 1 Thessalonians at this time in his journeys, around 50 A.D. But, the Rema is not used in 1 Thessalonians.

I got another check in my spirit by the Holy Spirit here; for in the two earliest manuscripts Codex Vaticaius 325/Sinitiaus 350 A.D, contains James, which is written about 50 A.D., and the rest of the general Epistles are placed after Acts. So, they were moved by Jerome in his Latin Vulgate translation because he was trying to carry out Constantine's efforts to stop the Jews from worshipping on Sabbath. These are some of the most "Jewish" writings in the NT, and they must be restored back to the proper place in NT.

 James [Greek: Jacob] did not use the Rema Word, but he has a wonderful statement about Hebrew theology in 1:1 which is "James bondservant [slave] of God and of the Lord Jesus Christ". This shows the very important idea in Judaic/Hebraic theology that it was A/Y who was in Jesus Christ the Messiah reconciling the world and us unto Himself, [see 2 Corinthians 5:18-21].

One of the most importance statements by James, and that was taught by his elder brother Jesus Christ, is: "If, however, you are fulfilling the royal [concordance: "Law of our King"] law according to the Scripture, 'You shall love your neighbor as Yourself, you are doing well." [James 2:8] The Torah in [Leviticus 19:18] taught us to love our neighbor, but Jesus Christ taught us by the power of the Holy Spirit we must also love our enemies in Matthew 5:44. We must have A/Y love poured out in our hearts by the H.S. before we can do this. [See Romans 5:5]

Peter, in his first Epistle, used Rema one time in 1:25, as he quoted Isaiah 40:6ff: "But the Word [Rema] of the Lord [A/Y] endures forever. And this is the Word which was preached [preached as good news to you the same as Romans.10:8 which we are preaching] to you." This is why all of our preaching/teaching must be the DeBarim/Remata Words of A/Y because they endure forever. We are speaking to people who will endure forever, and we must preach the Debars/Remata Words that endures forever. It is A/Y forever DeBars/Remata Words for our forever/forever.

2 <u>Peter,</u> in Chapter 3: 2 concludes with this profound statement in the Greek: It says: ". . .to remember the words [Remata] having being previously spoken by the holy prophets and the commandments of the apostles of your Lord and Saviour." This shows how the Holy Prophets in the FC and the apostles of our Lord and Saviour in the NT spoke the [Debars/Remata] of A/Y our Saviour/our Lord. We <u>must</u> speak.

<u>Jude</u> is identified as a slave of Jesus Christ, and brother of James 1:1. So much for the false theory that Jesus Christ did not have any brothers/sisters! Matthew says in 13: 556a "Is not this the carpenter's son? Is not His mother called Mary, and His brothers, James and Joseph and Simon, and Jude? v 56 And His sisters, are they not all with us?" Jude, in verse 17 says: "But you, beloved, ought to remember the words [Remata] that were spoken beforehand by the apostles of our Lord Jesus Christ." Jude reduces this down to the Apostles who beforehand spoke the Words [Remata] of our A/Y Jesus Christ Messiah which refers to the Gospels written later.

His greatest words tell us how to keep ourselves from causing divisions in the Body of Jesus Christ in verse 19. It says: "These are the ones who cause divisions, worldly minded [concordance: "merely natural"] devoid [not having] the Spirit." O how many Churches/lives have been destroyed because preacher/people/members did not have the H.S!!

Jude tells us in verse 20 how to keep the Love of A/Y. It says: "But you, beloved, <u>building</u> yourselves upon on your most holy faith, <u>praying</u> in the Holy spirit, <u>keep</u> yourselves in the Love of God, <u>waiting</u> anxiously for the mercy of our Lord Jesus Christ to eternal life." This building/praying/waiting in the Holy Spirit is a present active participle which means a continuous action. But "keep" is an aorist, past tense as also it is used in Ephesians 6:18.

So, the beloved Paul said 1 Thessalonians 5:17 "Pray without ceasing." Some doubt if our prayers are not in the Holy Spirit if they are really prayers and not just the repeating of empty words.

<u>Now,</u> we are following A.T. Robertson's outline in WPOTNT of Paul's letters in Volume 4, which are: 1 & 2 Thessalonians, 1 & 2 Corinthians, Galatians, Romans, Philippians, Philemon, Colossians, Ephesians, 1 Timothy, Titus, and 2 Timothy. See my outline on a Holy Spirit Guide to Reading/ Studying the New Testament, **[Addendum]** and see how they are related to Acts 18:5b where "Paul began devoting himself completely to the word [wrote 1 & 2 Thessalonians]."

<u>Now</u> we will look at a sidebar which is in 1 <u>Corinthians</u> 11:24-25, which the Holy Spirit spoke to me with a loud roar, and He said you have overlooked the most important part of <u>The</u> <u>New</u> <u>Covenant</u>. This is how Jesus Christ observed the Passover and established the order of the Lord's Supper according to Paul. Recorded in verse 23b, "He took bread, And when He had given thanks, He broke it and said, 'This is My Body, which is for you; do this in remembrance of Me.' " And, v25: "This cup is <u>The</u> <u>New</u> <u>Covenant</u> in My blood: do this, as often as you drink it, in remembrance of Me."

Paul had already told the 1 Corinthians in 5:7c-8 what to do. It says: "For Christ our Passover also has been sacrificed, v8 Therefore let us celebrate the <u>Feast: [Passover, Pentecost, And Sukkot tabernacle which</u>

are the 'Chaggin [Holy Days of Joy]' Holy feast of A'Y in Deuteronomy 16:16], not with old leaven, nor with the leaven of malice [A.T. Robertson: vicious disposition] and wickedness [again 'evil deed'], but with the unleavened bread of sincerity [again 'holding up to the light'] and truth." [So, "unconcealed," "not hidden"]

Paul concludes in 1 Corinthians 11:31-32, "But if we judge ourselves rightly, we will not be judged, v32 but, when we are judged, we are disciplined by the Lord so that we will not be condemned along with the World." We are given the opportunity to judge ourselves each time that we receive the Lord's Supper, [See 11:27-30], but if we do not judge ourselves A/Y Himself will judge us.

Paul talks about personal examination in verse 28: "But a man must examine himself." If we do not examine ourselves, the Holy Spirit will search us." 1 Corinthians 2:10b says "For the Spirit searches all things, even the depths of God." So, we must examine our conscience with the aid of the Holy Spirit [Romans 9:1] before we partake of the Lord's Supper. When we do not A/Y Himself will judge us for we are going to be judged one way or another. So, Let us judge ourselves rightly/and confess our sins before we partake.

2 Corinthians 12:4 gives a new insight into the use of Rema which is: "[I] was caught up into paradise and heard inexpressible words [Remata] which a man is not permitted to speak." I had to consult the Greek which says: "That He was caught into paradise and heard unspeakable words [Remata], which it is not permissible for a man to speak." So, when we hear all the visions that people tell, most are what Jeremiah 23:32 says, " 'Behold, I [A/Y] am against those who prophesied false dreams,' declares the Lord, 'and led My People astray

by their <u>falsehood</u> and <u>reckless boasting</u>.' " This is a clear statement and shows what falsehood are and do because they are reckless boasting of the individual. There are true visions and dreams, but many are not permissible to be spoken. The Holy Spirit has to speak them, in order for the visions/dreams to be the Living DeBars/Remata of A/Y.

2 Corinthians 13:1 informs: "This is the third time I [Paul] am coming to you, Every fact [Rema] is [shall be] to be confirmed by the testimony [mouth] of two or three witnesses." So, we see again that every Rema must be confirmed by the mouth of two or three witnesses. No one can claim that what he/she says is from Christ dwelling in them, and therefore they cannot be questioned by anyone. This is foolishness and show how error has <u>crept</u> into and has <u>hurt</u> the Prophetic Ministries rather than people being helped to believe in the true prophet and prophecies [prophecies not despise. [1Thessalonians 5:20]   Also, it cannot be denied that noteworthy miracles happen. [Acts 4:16]

Others in the Messianic Body are to discern all messages in tongues and all prophesy to see if the Holy Spirit is speaking noteworthy miracles or not. If they are not happening according to Scripture, then it is a man speaking and not the Holy Spirit.   [See 1 Corinthians 14:29]

See Chapter 15.

CHAPTER 15

We are continuing our discussion of Paul's use of the Rema word, and he does not use it but eight times. The two in 2 Corinthians 13:1; 14:1, and the two times in <u>Romans</u> 10:8.

Notice that in Romans 10:8 he is quoting Deuteronomy 30:14 which says "But what does it say? 'The word [Rema] is near you, in your mouth and in your heart' —that is the word [Rema] of faith which we are preaching." This gives meaning to the word "Rema:" **The <u>Word</u> of <u>faith</u>**. When A/Y speaks these words of faith to us we receive the power to <u>say</u> or <u>do</u> what He wills.

> *When A/Y speaks these "words of faith" to us, we receive the power to <u>say</u> or <u>do</u> what He wills.*

A personal note: Back in 1953, I had been praying for six months to be able to quit smoking, and I had tried every effort known to man to quit, but I was not able to quit. I was on a mountain in Lindale Ga, praying. Smoking was affecting my voice after I preached two times on Sunday, and as I was praying to A/Y, He spoke to me and said, "A preacher without a voice is like a car without a motor it is not good for anything but the junk yard."

I cried out, "O, A/Y help me! If you will provide the grace I will provide the man." As, I was driving down around a curve the Spirit said to me in a whisper, "Throw the cigarettes out the window." I took a pence box of matches and a pack of cigarette and threw them out the window of the car. When they got at eye level it was like a picture was snapped in my mind, and the desire and addiction of cigarette left me immediately, and I have never wanted or smoked another one. As I am writing this it has been 60 years ago, and I am still able to preach/teach the DeBarim /Remata Gospel Words like a "holy roller."

The Rema word of faith is explained clearly in Romans 10:17 which is: "So Faith comes by hearing, and hearing by the word [Rema] [concerning Messiah] of Christ." This is what happens every time someone hear A/Y speak by the Ruach ha Kodesh these DeBarim/Remata Words directly/indirectly through a messenger: they Empower/Work.

A.T. Robertson said: "A Hebraistic and vernacular use of rhema (something said) as something done." (END) 88   This is as good of interpretation of the DeBar/Rema Words as I have been able to find anywhere. A/Y says it: it is done!

One of the greatest proclamations in the whole NT is found in Romans 10:18, which says: "But I say, 'surely they have never heard, have they? Indeed they have; their voice has gone out into all the earth, and their words [Remata] to the end of the world [inhabited earth].' " Paul quotes Psalms 19:4, which shows what good Judaic/Hebraic theology is all about. It is about A/Y's Sovereign Will and Way. All hear/All will have to give an account to A/Y for His DeBarim/Remata Words which they have indeed heard. This explains the bold statement by Paul in Romans 1:20:

> *"For since the creation of the world His invisible attributes, His eternal Power and [D]divine nature, have been clearly seen, being understood through what has been made, so that they are without excuse."*

In Romans 2:1a, in the Greek, we learn: "Wherefore inexcusable thou art, O Man everyone judging." This is exactly what Jesus Christ taught in Matthew 7: 1-2 which says, "Do not judge, so that you will not be judged. v 2 For in the way you judge, you will be judged; and by your standard [by what measure you measure], it will be measured unto you." This warns us about our judgmental attitudes and our "measures" out to others. We are bringing severe judgment and measure upon ourselves. I am so thankful A/Y did not tell us to judge others. Jesus Christ did say that you would know a tree by what kind of fruit it bore, but there is a vast different between knowing different kinds of fruit and knowing a person's heart.

 Only A/Y knows the heart as it is taught in Jeremiah 17:9f, and in Acts 1:24 which says: "And, they said, 'You, Lord, who knows the hearts of all men, show which one of these two You have chosen.' " They were doing things the old way based upon Psalms 85:2, which was not the Way that A/ Y chose for the New/Living way of been led by the Holy Spirit.

At least they knew the Bible, which most believers do not read or study, which causes so many errors in belief and doctrines. [See Mark 12:24-28] We have already looked at this verse, but it cannot be said enough; that the Bible is the most sold and loved book in the world;

and, it is the most unread and unstudied book in the world. Mark 12:27 says, "He is not the God of the dead, but of the living: You are greatly mistaken." "It is the Power of God unto Salvation unto the Jew first and the Greek." [Romans 1:16]

So, Satan's greatest weapon is to keep the believer from reading and studying the Bible because in it is the Power of A/Y being revealed, and the Believer will be healed in his/her inner person when we do what James taught in 5:16 which reads: "Therefore, confess yours sins to one another and pray for one another so that [hina in order that: causes] you may be healed.' Notice, it says sins and not faults as the KJV says.

> . . .the taking of the helmet of salvation . . . is necessary to receiving "the sword of the Spirit!"

In Ephesians 5:26, Paul shows how we are to wash ourselves in the Rema Word. What is amazing about this is where we find this gem – right in the section about the Bride of Christ [the Church] which says: "So that [a hina clause "in order that" causes] He might sanctify Her, having cleaned Her by the washing of the water with the Word [Rema]." How about that? A washing of water with the Rema Word! Continuously, being washed by the Water of the Rema Word! What was the cultural more of Paul's day for the bride on her wedding day? She spent the whole day, even the whole week or many months making herself ready for her wedding .

The Messianic Body is the Bride of Messiah, and we should spend the rest of our lives after we have been born from above by the Spirit and after we have received the Baptism of the Holy Spirit from our risen and exalted Messiah [Luke 3:15] washing ourselves in the Rema Words.

There is a beautiful parable and warning by Jesus Christ about what we should be doing while we are waiting for the Bridegroom. It is found in Matthew 25:1-13. Read it and be prepared to meet the Bridegroom when He Comes. Many say that they are waiting for the Bridegroom, but about half of them are unprepared for His coming by not having oil in their lamps which is the Holy Spirit. According to verse 13: "Be on the alert then, for you do not know the day or the hour" [of His coming]. Those on high/full alert should be continuously washing themselves in the Word [Rema] and being filled with the Holy Spirit. Ephesians 5:18 says, "And do not get drunk with wine, for [in which is] that is dissipation, but be filled [but be you continuously being filled with the Holy Spirit] with the Spirit."

Paul in 1 Thessalonians 5:8, mentions the amour of A/Y. But, in Ephesians 6:10-17, he explains about putting on the whole Amour of God. "Finally, be strong in the Lord and in the strength of His might." Then, he tells why in verses 11-12, and in verse 13 he tells us therefore to take up the whole Amour, and in verse 16, again to take up the shield of faith. But in verse 17 he changes the verb and it is not to take up but to receive.

The Expositor's Greek New Testament, (TEGNT) on the Book of Ephesians 6:17 says: "The verb has its proper sense here, not merely 'take,' but 'receive,' i.e., as a gift from the Lord, a thing provided and offered by Him." (END) 89   This distinction is necessary for – the taking of the helmet of salvation is necessary to receiving "the sword of the Spirit who is the Rema of God."

In Abbot's *Commentary on Romans*, Markus Barth is quoted saying, "The rema word of God is given by the Holy Spirit." So, this tells us that it is the Spirit who is the Rema Word of God and His sword [SEE: Hebrews 4:12] (END) 90

Again, 'TEGNT, says, "Some strangely make the 'O' refer to pneumatos, meaning: 'the Spirit who is the word [Rema] of God." (END) 91
This is the only way that it can be correctly translated. The Spirit who is the Word [Debars /Remata of Yah] our God.

This ties the Spirit, who must always come first, to the Words, but always before the Words come. The two are tied together in an iron clad unbreakable bond. The Spirit and the Remata Words are tied together like the Spirit and DeBars Words are tied together in the OT in the CJB in Proverbs 1:23, which says: "Repent at **My** reproof – I will pour out **My** spirit to [on] you, I will make **My** Words [DeBars] known to you." This gives a clear statement of how and when a relationship between the Ruach and the Debars comes about in the OT, and it is no different in the NT. That is the Holy Spirit who speaks/reveals the [Remata] Words of A/Y to us and works Miracles.

It is strange that Paul does not use the Rema Word but eight times in all of his Epistles, but because of his knowledge of the DeBar in the OT, it is so important that he explains fully the Remata in Romans 10:8-17. "It is that Rema Word of Faith which we are preaching." Verse 17 says: "Faith comes by hearing, and hearing by the [Rema] Word of God." So, we must wash ourselves continuously/daily in the Rema Word of God. [Ephesians 6:18]

We now will look at <u>John's</u> Gospel in Chapter 16!

CHAPTER 16

DR. A.T. Robertson discusses in Volume 5 of his WPOTNT the Books of John and Hebrews. We will follow this same order.

In his introduction he says, "If Luke's Gospel is the most beautiful, John's is supreme in its height and depth and reach of thought. The language of **the Fourth Gospel** has the clarity of a spring, but we are not able to sound the bottom of the depths. Lucidity and profundity challenge and charm us as we linger over it."   (END)   92

In **John** 3:31-36 we find the first **spring**. Read the whole and look closely at verse 34, which says "For, He whom God has sent speaks the Words [Remata] of God; for [because He does not give the Spirit by measure] He gives the Spirit without measure." This so important because it says in Acts 2:17, " 'And, it shall be in the last days', God says, 'that I will pour forth **of** My Spirit on all mankind [flesh].' " Many today have forgotten the [**of**] [the KJV got it right] , and that as I argued earlier, that some people think that they can speak the Rema Word of A/Y because Christ dwells within them without anyone questioning them.

A/Y pours out His Spirit upon Jesus Christ the Messiah without measure. The Anointing One in Hebrews is Messiah, as in Greek; it is Christ. We can be anointed with the Holy Spirit as it says in 1 John 2:20, 27, but it is only **of** His Spirit but not without measure, as it was upon Jesus Christ the Messiah.

The difference is in the vessels, because Messiah was the sinless Son of A/Y, and we are sons/daughters of A/Y if we are led [driven Mark I:12 says] by The Holy Spirit.   Romans 8:14 says, "For all who are being led ["**driven**" = Kaseman] by the Spirit of God, these are sons [and daughters of God." And, as 2 Corinthians 6: 18 says, " 'And I will be a Father to you, and you shall be sons and daughters to Me', says the Lord Almighty.' " Thanks to A/Y that daughters were included, because some men want to exclude them. But not 1 Peter 3:7-11, which says, "Since she is a woman; show her honor as a fellow heir of the grace of life, so that yours prayers will not be hindered."   Verse 11b says: ". . .he must seek peace and purse it."

The truth is that we are all being driven by the Holy Spirit, or we are being driven by the lust of our flesh as it says in Romans 6:18: "And, having been freed from sin, you became slaves of righteousness." We have no other choice, and we must choose by which one we are going to be driven. See Romans 8:12a: "So then, brethren, we are under obligation, [debtor as 1:14]," which the NASB translates it as obligation in both places because they could not believe that they/we are slaves to the flesh or to the Holy Spirit]. I love the saying in the Black Church when someone is preaching – they will say, "Make it plain Brother!" And, just so, Paul has made it plain. I am trying my best to make it as plain as I can.

There is a profound spring or teaching about the scriptures in John 5:39-47. Verse 39f says: "You search the scriptures because you think that in them you have eternal life; it is these that testify about Me; v40 and you are unwilling to come to Me so that you may have life." This is one of the most amazing statements to me in the NT because some people today search the scriptures to argue about them, but they will not receive Jesus Christ/Messiah as their Saviour and have eternal life, and they will not sanctify Him in their hearts as Lord [1 Peter 3:15] and have life more abundantly [John 10:10]. Thanks A/Y.

In John 5:46-47, there is a comparison between Moses and Jesus Christ. It says: "For if you believed Moses, you would believe Me, for he wrote about Me. v47 But if you do not believe his writings, how will you believe My Words [Remata]?" This has a double edged meaning to it. If we do not believe the DeBarim taught by Moses in Deuteronomy 18:18 about the first coming of the Messiah then we will not believe the NT about His second Coming.

We also will not believe about the Jewish roots of the NT, and we will be teaching/practicing "replacement theology" rather than fulfilled Judaic/Hebraic theology Romans 10:4, which says: "For Christ [Messiah] is the end [con Causes/Purpose/Goal] of the law for righteousness to everyone who believes." Here [Greek word: "Telos" means cause, purpose, and goal and not end [KJV]. Jesus Christ Messiah is the Causes/ Purpose/Goal of all Torahs.

For the whole counsel of Adonai/YHWH must be preached and taught. Act 20:27 says, "For I [Paul] did not shrink from declaring to you the whole purpose [counsel] of God." We have a lot of preachers today who shrink back from declaring the whole counsel of A/Y just as there has always been and always will be some. [See: Isaiah 30:10.]

Another crystal clear spring, about the Spirit and the Rema Word, is found in 6:63. We have discussed this verse fully before. Read/memorize it.

Then, another crystal clear spring about Cephas' confession of the Rema Word is found in 6:67-71. John declares in verse 67: "So Jesus said to the twelve, 'You do not want to go away also, do you?' v68 [And] Simon Peter answered Him, 'Lord, to whom shall we go? You have words [remata] of eternal life.' " To whom shall we go Jesus Christ Messiah because You are the Logos [Gospel][See: John 1:1], and You have the words [Remata] of eternal life. This is what everybody [really wants] needs more than anything else in life, but they will not come to Jesus Christ to receive the gift of eternal life from Him. [See: 5:40]

John 7:2, 37-39 is a side bar that we cannot pass by without stopping and drinking from the crystal clear spring, which will become an artesian well turning into gushing rivers. The TLV gives it this way in 7:2: "The Jewish feast of Tabernacles was near." This is the celebration of Sukkot. Verses 37-39 states, "On the last greatest day of the Feast, Yeshua stood up and cried out loudly, 'If anyone is thirsty, let him come (subjunctive in the Greek – "keep on coming") to Me and drink. Whoever believes in Me, as the Scripture says, out of his innermost being will flow rivers of living water.' Now He said this about the Ruach, whom those who trusted in Him were going to receive; for the Ruach was not yet given, since Yeshua was not yet glorified."

The Greek must be translated ["If anyone thirst, let him keep coming to Me and [keep on] drinking"]. This subjunctive translation is given in the concordance of the NASB which requires a continuous action by us, and it <u>must</u> be translated this way to show it correctly.

This shows why so many who have received the baptism of the Holy Spirit dry up, since they do not <u>keep</u> on <u>coming</u> and <u>keep</u> on <u>drinking.</u> Therefore, Messiah cannot "be being" Glorified in them/their body. This is also confirmed in 2 Peter 3:18 TLV which says: "And keep growing in grace and knowledge of our Lord and Savior Yeshua the Messiah." No growth! No fruit, because the fruit always grows on the new growth.

So, if we are not drinking/ growing we will not be bearing any fruit as a Believer. We are commanded by Jesus Christ to bear fruit. The reason is so that He will be being Glorified in our body. [See: John 15:5; and See: 1 Corinthians 5:20, which says: "For you have been bought with a price: therefore glorify God in your body," and not just in your spirit and soul but glorify Messiah in His Body [Soma 1 Corinthians 3:16; 2 Corinthians 6:16; Ephesians 2:21f note: v16, 21] a Holy Temple "naos Holy of Holiness' and v22 a dwelling of God [A/Y in the Spirit] which is our body <u>here</u> and <u>now</u>. He Rules/Reigns.

As Romans 8:30 says: ". . .and these, whom He predestined, He also called; and these whom He called, He also justified; and these whom He justified, He also glorified." [He called **ALL** according to Jewish Theology in Deuteronomy 30:19, 1 Timothy 2:4, and 2 Peter 3:9, Because, A/Y, our Savior desires all men to be saved and to come the full knowledge {means to receive the baptism of the Holy Spirit, Luke 3:15} of the truth]. There is also this being Glorified now in our body by

His presence as well as the complete glorification of body [Romans 8: 23] in the future for All Believers.   Hallelujah!

There is a beautiful insight into Jesus Christ's teaching in John 8:20, 47 which says: "These words [Remata] He spoke in the treasury, as He taught in the Temple; and no one seized Him, because His hour had not yet come." This shows that Jesus Christ spoke these Remata in the treasury while He was teaching in the Temple as was His custom. Then verse 47 says, and warns us about the Rema: "He who is of God hears the words [Remata] of God; for this reason you do not hear them, because you are not of God." We spoke early about the Debars/Remata are only heard and believed by the believer, and this verse confirms that it is only when we are being/obedience to A/Y that we can <u>hear</u> and <u>do</u> these Words.

> *"Death itself is not so bad, because we all will die, but it is the judgment that is awaiting us, that gives us great concern and motivates us all to try to live Godly and Holy lives."*

Another clear distinction between the Logos Word and the Rema Word as was given in Acts 10:44 is shown here: "A division occurred among the Jews because of these words [Logos]. v20 Many of them were saying [lego], 'He has a demon and is insane. Why do you listen to Him? v21 Others were saying, 'These are not the saying [Rema] of one who is demon possessed. A demon cannot open the eyes of the blind, can he?' "

This gives a clear picture and illustration of the difference between the Logos and the Rema; and it also gives the clear word of a man/woman who is allowing A/Y to speak these Remata Words that open the hearts [Luke 4:18-19] and proclaim release to them.

A summary of much of what John has been saying about Jesus Christ's words is found in 12:46-48. Jesus said all along: "I have come as Light into the world, so that everyone who believes in Me will not remain in darkness, v47 If anyone hears My saying [Remata] and does not keep them, I do not judge them; for I did not come in the world to judge, but to save the world. v48 He who rejects Me and does not receive My sayings [Remata], has one who judges him; the word [Logos] I spoke is what will judge him at the last days."

The Logos Gospel and the Remata Words which Messiah spoke by/through the Holy Spirit will judge all of us at the last days. As, Hebrews 9:27 says in the KJV: "And as It is appointed unto man once to die, but after this the judgment." Death itself is not so bad because we all will die, but it is the judgment that is awaiting us that gives us great concern and motivates us all to try to live Godly and Holy lives.

In 14:10, here, we come to one of the most important parts of John's whole book. In chapters 14 & 17, he tells what and why we must hear the Rema Word of A/Y. "Do you not believe that I am in the Father; and the Father is in Me? The words [Remata] that I say to you I do not speak on My own initiative, but *__the Father dwelling in Me does His Works__* ." [TIV] In this we see a new revelation Jesus Christ gives about the Remata Words of A/Y; for it is the Father dwelling and speaking in/through us by the Holy Spirit: Adonai/Yah is at Work in/ through us.

This explains why we must allow the Holy Spirit to speak the Remata Words and Work in/through us.

When we hear anyone preaching/prophesying we all must discern whether it is a man speaking, or if it is the Holy Spirit of A/Y speaking in them. If it is the Holy Spirit the WORDS will be allowing the Father to do His Works. [See: Philippians 2:12-13]. Abba, Father do the Works of Your Kingdom in/ through us! HalleluYah!!!!!!

One of the most important statements that need to be repeated again and again about "abiding in Me" [words of Jesus Christ] is in this whole section found in 15:7: "If you abide in Me [Messiah] and My Words [Remata] abide in you, ask whatever you wish, and it will be done." This must be understood in light of Psalms 119:72: "The Torah from Your mouth is better to me, than thousands of gold and silver pieces." None of this "name it and claim it" **heresy** that is being preached today by many and on T.V. HalleluYah.

We go now to Chapter 17.

CHAPTER 17

___

In John 14:13, this statement is made: "Whatever you ask in My name, that I will do so that [here is the unique Greek clause "in order that" which causes things to happen] the Father might be glorified in the Son." We hear so many people say "in the Name of Jesus" based upon this verse, and we do not see the things that they are praying for come into reality, or what they are saying happen. Why?

John 15:7 gives the answer: "If you abide in Me [the Vine] and My Word [Remata] abides in you; ask whatever you wish, and it will be done for You." This double abiding protects the Name and the Glory of Adonai/Yah.

When we are abiding in Him and His Remata Words are abiding in us, we are so full of His Glory that we are going to fall on our face and give Glory to His Holy Name. We will not be asking for foolish things or for things to heap upon our lust. In James 4:3 in the KJV it says: "You ask and receive not, because you ask amiss, that you may consume it upon your lusts."

Here in both John and James is that good Judaic Hebraic Theology, and no wonder some wanted to omit James from the Bible. But, it is not just James who is so Judaic Hebraic, but it is all the NT writers who are all completely Judaic/Hebraic.

I remember when I first received the baptism of the Holy Spirit that I would go into the prayer room with all my requests, and I would get caught up in His Presence and I would Worship and Praise Him for two or three hours. I would forget about all the requests that I had, and when I came to myself, many times as I was leaving the Prayer room, I would say: "Abba, Father You know about all the requests and all the needs please take care of all of them."

I had the assurance that He would do it. Read 1 Thessalonians 5:23-24 in the KJV. "The very God of peace will sanctify you wholly, and I [Paul] pray God your whole spirit and soul and body be preserved blameless unto ["In the presence" is in the Greek] the coming of the Lord Jesus Christ." When I first saw this many would say He does not do that now, but after someone had said that to me the Holy Spirit revealed verse 24 to me, "Faithful is He that calleth you, and He will do it." [KJV] It was amazing then and now when this happens. Yes, it still does happen. HalleluYah to A/Y.

One time, when I had preached and bragged about Him doing this in my life, A/Y said this to me early the next morning. "You left out the most important part!" And, I had to go back to the scriptures to find out what I had left out. It was/is verse 25: "Brethren, pray for us" and, when I saw this it took away all the bragging about what had happened to me, and I cried out "Brethren, pray for me. It's all about A/Y and not about me, who is a nobody." [See and read 1 Corinthians 1:7]

John, Chapter 17 is the true Lord's Prayer, and we should read and pray it often. In 17:6-12 Jesus Christ prays for all His disciples who are in the world, and verse 8 says: "For the words [Remata] which You gave Me I have given to them; and they received them and truly understand that I came forth from You, and they believed that You sent Me." What a revealing statement this is about the Rema Word because it reveals that A/Y sent Jesus Christ Messiah into the World.

When we allow the Holy Spirit to speak the DeBars/Remata Words in/through us the world will believe that A/Y has sent us into the world and that He is performing signs, wonders, and miracles in and through us.

We now go to the book of **Hebrews.** What a wonderful statement: a book in the NT written to the Jewish people in the Diaspora [according to the sowing of seeds: A/Y sowed the World with His DeBars Words through Moses and in the Jewish People (see Romans 9:16)]. Wow! I have never <u>read</u> or <u>heard</u> anyone who translated this this way before, and they who are called the Hebrews. A/Y is now sowing His DeBars/Remata Words in/through His Messianic Body of Jews and Gentiles. They must **not** have been replaced by the Messianic Body of Jesus Christ because they have a book written to them.

Many scholars are amazed that Hebrews and 1 & 2 Peter are so much alike, and they say that whoever wrote Hebrews must have known about Peter's Epistles. We know who wrote his epistles because it says in 1 Peter 5:12: "Through Silvanus [Silas in Hebrew], our faithful brother (for so I regard/consider him '), I have written to you briefly, exhorting and testifying that this is the true grace of God. Stand firm in it!"

It is possible from this internal evidence of both Peter's Epistles and Hebrews that Silas also wrote Hebrews? It says in 13:22-23: "But I urge you, brethren, bear [listen to] this word [the] word of exhortation, for I have written to you briefly. V 23 take notice [know] that our brother Timothy has been released, with whom, if he comes soon, I will see you." Timothy and Silas were with Paul most of the time from the beginning of his second missionary journey.

This should not be a surprise to us because we know what it says in the Greek, in Acts 15:22-29: "Judah, being called Barsabas and Silas men leading among the brothers, v23 writing through the hand of them." Dr. A. T. Robertson says: "And, they wrote." The Greek is a first aorist participle, according Robertson, so we know that Silas was a writer because he wrote this letter found in Acts 15, and 1 Peter. He also heard all Paul's sermons and read all his Letters. Also It says in Hebrews 13:23 TLV, "Knowing that our brother Timothy has been released. If he comes soon, I will visit you with him." (END)   93

"Rema" is used four times in the book of Hebrews, and in 1:3 it says: "And He [who being Jesus Christ] is the radiance of His glory and the exact representation of His nature, and upholds [Greek: "Bearing" present activity] all things by the [Rema] Word of His Power." This shows what has been said in "all [the whole] of the Holy Bible" about all the DeBars/ Remata Words of Adonia/Yah. They are His Present/Power/Event in action. They were/are His Power, and His Power is <u>upholding</u> all things in the universe, and is <u>upholding</u> all things in the Messianic Body of Jesus Christ, Messiah our Lord, and is <u>upholding</u> all things in our bodies and lives, if we allow Him. HalleluYah.

This is shown clearly in Genesis 1:1, where it says:

"In the beginning God created [Bara] the Heavens and the earth, v2 The earth was formless [waste and emptiness and no order] and void [no meaning], and darkness [no light] was on the surface [face of] of the deep, and the Spirit of God was moving [hovering] over the surface [face of] the waters."

This is the most graphic picture that I have ever seen of our lives when we are not being saved, and we are not being continuously filled with the Holy Spirit, which brings order, purpose, and light to our lives. [See Ephesians 5:19] Halleleujah!

Hebrews 6:4-6 is awesome; which says:

"For it is impossible for those who once were enlightened—having tasted of the heavenly gift and become partakers of the Ruach haKodesh, and having tasted the good [Rema] word of God, and the Power of the age to come, v 6 and then having fallen away, it is impossible to renew them again unto repentance, since [while] they again crucify to themselves the Son of God and put Him to open shame." TLV

Verse 5 says, "Yes, you have tasted the good [Debar s.Joshua 21:45, 23:14: Jeremiah 29:10 Rema] Word of God, and the Power of the coming Age." Yes, we can taste the good DeBar/Rema Word of God and the power the coming age <u>now</u>. Ephesians 1:3 has "spiritual blessings in the heavenly [note places is not in the text] in Christ," and in 2:4-6, it says: v4 "but God" and, v6 says: "and [God] raised us up with Him, and seated us with Him in the heavenly [places again not in the text] in Christ Jesus." What more could anyone want than to be able to sit together in the heavenly in Messiah? You can see/know the ones who are experiencing the heavenly in Jesus Christ Messiah in their eyes/their lives here/<u>now</u>.

And, now we will discuss Hebrews 5:6, because it has caused much controversy about one losing his/her salvation. First, it is not about salvation but it is about sanctification. Salvation in Hebrews chapter 1-5 is unconditional because of what Jesus Christ did for us on the cross and it is eternal life [Romans 6:23], but chapters 6-12 are about sanctification, which is always conditional, depending upon our <u>disobedience</u> or our <u>obedience</u>. See/Read Act 5:32 which we have already discussed, and it says very clearly that A/Y gives His Holy Spirit only to them that obey Him. We have eternal Salvation by grace through faith, and we can continually be being sanctified by the Holy Spirit by grace through faith and become one with Him. In Hebrews 2: 11, the Greek says: "For both the [one] sanctifying and the one being sanctified [are] all one." How about that? He not only is a Power in us: Acts 1:8; but He will keep on sanctifying us as one, if we keep on washing ourselves daily in the water of Rema Word, Ephesians 5:26.

> *"A false doctrine is worse than a moral failure."*
>
> *-rodney howard brown*
>
> ———◆———
>
> *Because you will always be going back to that false doctrine believing the same thing, but a moral failure can be confessed and be forgiven.*

Although 11:3 almost repeats 1:3, it gives us some additional information about the Rema Word of A/Y. It says: "By faith we understand that the worlds [ages] were prepared by the [Rema] word of God, so that [anytime you see "so that" it is always a hina purpose clause "in order that"] what is seen was make out of things which are visible." A/Y always creates out of nothing what is visible, and that is why now faith is so important/necessary as Chapter 11:1 says.

12:19a gives the final statement about Rema in Hebrew which is in the KJV: "And the sound of a trumpet, and the voice of the [Remata] words." The Remata Words are the voice [phome] of Adonai/Yah speaking to us like a trumpet directly or indirectly. If He does not speak the DeBars/Remata then there will be no creating, saving, deliverance, and healing. However, when He does speak, all these will be happening in us. Let Him speak to you daily, by washing yourselves in the water of the Rema Word, Ephesians 5:26.

1 Peter 1:25 has a bold statement about the Rema. **Look,** how this writer uses the Logos in v23b: "You have been born again—not from perishable seed but imperishable—through the living and enduring word of God," and in v25: "But the Word {Rema} of the Lord endures forever, and this is the Word that was proclaimed as Good News to you." [TLV] The enduring Logos is the Gospel, and the enduring Rema is Living/Power of the Living Adonai/YHWH upholding [Hebrews 1:3] / creating/operating the Power of God in Us.

2 Peter 3:1 has a profound statement about what we are to do, "In both, I am trying to stir you up by way of a **reminder** to wholesome thinking to **remember** the Words [Remata] previously proclaimed by

the holy prophets and the commanding of our Lord and Savior through your emissaries, TLV."

Judah, the brother of Jesus Christ agrees and confirms Peter's statement about remembering the Rema in v17: "But you, loved ones, ought to remember the Words [Remata] previously proclaimed by emissaries of our Lord Jesus Christ the Messiah." [TLV] It is high/pass time that we do some wholesome/sober **thinking** and **remembering** the DeBarim/Remata Words of Adonai/ YHWH. The whole Words of the Word of A/Y found in the Bible.

Revelation 14:13 has one of the greatest statements about the death of a believer in the Bible, and it has almost been lost because of the so called "Faith Healers."

The "Double Fire Baptizing Holiness People" says that because our Souls were completely healed by what Messiah did on the Cross; that our bodies were also completely healed, and we could live without sickness or sin in our bodies. This is a false assumption, because it contradicts [Romans 7:7-25; 8:23] the true Judaic/Hebraic Theology, which Paul taught in Romans 7:7ff. Read through and note what v25 says: "Thanks be to God through Jesus Christ our Lord! So then, on the one hand I Myself with My mind am serving the law of God, but on the other hand, with the flesh, the law of sin." Any Western doctrines that contradict this true Judaic/Hebraic Theological doctrine of Paul, the slave of Messiah, is a wrong assumption.

Rodney Howard Brown, on his program *The Great Awakening,* on The Christian Television Network, on January 6, 2013, said something that was a revelation to me: "A false doctrine is worse than a moral failure." Because you will always be going back to that false doctrine believing the same thing, but a moral failure can be confessed and be forgiven [see 1 John 1:9] (p. s. I had to forgive a brother who had fallen] but we will not go back to that sin if we truly repented: repent means to turn the opposite direction from sin.

We have been praying for a brother who has cancer, and he was told that he had a <u>block</u> to his healing because of some unconfessed sin in his Life. Another said the reason that he was not healed was because he did not have enough faith. Both of these assumptions are wrong!

Paul gives the answer in Philippians 1:20 which says: "According to my earnest expectation and hope, that I will not be put to shame in anything, but that with all boldness, Christ will even now, as always, be exalted in my body whether by life or death." These above assumptions cause people who have cancer to be put to <u>shame</u> because they are made to feel that it is their fault rather than that Messiah can be exalted in their body even though they are not healed.

Look, what it says in Psalms 116:15 TLV brings freedom: "Precious in the sight of the Adonai is the death of His kedoshim (saints)." And Psalms 72:14 TLV says: "From oppression and violence he redeems their soul, for precious is their blood in his sight." These two verses bring comfort and joy during their sickness and homegoing.

We should be teaching people what James 5:13-16 says:

> v13 "If anyone among you is suffering? Then he must pray." v14 is very plan which says: "Is anyone among you sick? Then he must call for the elders of the church and they are to pray over him,

anointing [con. having anointing] with oil in the name of the Lord;
v15 and the prayers offered [con. of] faith will restore [con. save]
the one who is sick, and the Lord will raise him up, and if he has
committed sins, they will be forgiven him. v16 Therefore, confess
your sins to one another and pray for one another so that you may
be healed. The effective prayer [con. supplication] of a righteous
man can accomplish much."

<u>Colossians</u> has the Biblical answer to all suffering and sickness.
We find in Chapter 1:24: [In the Greek it says]: "Now, I rejoice in
my sufferings on behalf of you, and fill up the things lacking of the
affliction of Christ in the flesh of me on behalf of the body of Him,
which is the Church." He does not promise us that we will not
suffer or get sick, but He does promise that in some mystical way
it will be filling up the things lacking of the affliction of the
Messiah on behalf of His Body: His Church. Further, Colossians
1:24 gives people the <u>assurance,</u> rather than the <u>shame,</u> that we
need to be giving to people who are suffering and sick. It says:

". . .strengthened with all power according to His [con. the might
of His Glory] glorious might, for [con. unto all] the attaining of all
steadfastness and patience; [con. longsuffering patiently with Joy]
joyously."

Dr. A.T. Robertson says: "Hupomone is remaining under (hupomeno
burden with Patience) difficulties without succumbing, while
makrothumia (longsuffering) is the lone endurance that does not
retaliate, (Trench)."   (END)   94   A/Y was /is longsuffering with
Israel (Romans 9:22b) /Us, so that we should be longsuffering with
each other!!

Yahweh is our healer as Exodus 15:25 says, and some have the "charimata of healing," according to 1 Corinthians 12:9, 28, "but not all have it" according to v28 as some who have received it believe. It is only when our going to sleep in Jesus Christ exalts Him more than our being healed does that we can have our home going. Philippians 1:23b: "Having the desire to depart and be with Messiah, for that is very much better." Amen, thank You A/Y.

Paul, as Philippians 1: 21-22 says: "For to me, to live is Christ, and to die is gain." v. 22 [concordance: "But if I am to live on in the flesh, this will bring fruitful labor for me, then what shall I choose?"] I choose fruitful labor for You Yahweh: So that You will be Glorified in my body whether by life/death.

Now, read Revelation 14:13 and memorize it.

> "Then I heard a voice from heaven saying,   'Write: How fortunate are the dead—those who die in the Lord from now on!'
>
> 'Yes,' says the Ruach, 'that they may rest from their labors, for their deeds (works) follow   them.' "

This means we can receive Jesus Christ's Peace here and now, as John 14: 27 says: "Peace I leave with you; My Peace I give unto you; not as the world gives do I give to you. Do let not your heart be troubled, nor let it be fearful." This Shalom/Peace **passes** all Knowledge [Ephesians 3:19 TLV ". . .so you may be filled with all the fullness of God,"] even in our sickness and sleep in Jesus Christ Messiah in death.

Revelation 17:17 we see the final use of Rema in the NT which says: "For God has put it in their hearts to execute His purpose [Mind] by

181

[even to do one mind and to give] having a common purpose, and by giving their kingdom to the beast, until the words [Remata] of God be fulfilled." O, Praise Adonai/Yah because all His DeBars/Remata Words: His Will, Mind, Purpose and Goal will be fulfilled. Until then let us perfect Him by trying to live holy lives. And, let our witness be as Hebrews 11:40 TLV says, "Because God had provided [Foreseen] something better for us, so that only with us would they reach perfection." I believe that this can happen here and now as we are trying to perfect Adonai/Yah' Holiness [2 Corinthians 7:1] and honor our parents by the life that we are now living.

Amen, so be it A/Y.

Addendum 1

(In reference to the outline in Chapter 14, page 153)

A HOLY SPIRIT GUIDE

"TO READING AND STUDYING THE NEW TESTAMENT"

By: Billy Abney

I. Begin in Luke: The Gospel of the Holy Spirit
   A. Mark: Read the parallel passage in the Good News.
   B. Matthew
II. Read Acts of the Holy Spirit: Chapters 1-12 deals with the life of Peter and the Jerusalem Church, it has three books.
   A. Chapter 1:1-6:7 dated AD 30-35 The Word grew.
   B. Chapter 6:8-9:31 dated AD 35-40 The Church grew and multiplied.
   C. Chapter 9:32-12:24 dated 40-45 The Word grew and multiplied.
III. Read Acts chapters 13-28 which deals with the life of Paul and the Church at Antioch.
   A. Chapters 12:25-16:5 – AD 45-50   The Church grew.
   B. Chapters 16:6-19:20 – AD 50-55   The Word grew/prevailed.
      1. At Chapter 18:11
         a. 1 Thessalonians   50 AD
         b. 2 Thessalonians 51 AD

2. At Chapter 19:20
   a. 1 Corinthians 52 AD
   b. 2 Corinthians 53 AD
   c. Galatians 53 AD
   d. Romans   54 AD

C. Chapters 19:21-28:31 – AD 55-60
   1. At Chapter 24:27
      a. Philippians   55 AD
      b. Philemon   56 AD
      c. Colossians 57 AD
      d. Ephesians   57 AD

   2. Read the rest of Acts – Preached the Word unhindered.

      a. 1 Timothy   64 AD
      b. Titus   64 AD
      c. 2 Timothy   65 AD
      d. 1 Peter   65 AD
      e. 2 Peter   65 AD
      f. Hebrews   68 AD
      g. John's Gospel   68-70 AD
      h. The rest of the New Testament – The General Epistles
         to Revelation   68-70 AD

Billy Abney
1212 Gray Hwy
Apt 601
Macon, GA 31211

END NOTES (FINAL)

CHAPTER 1

1. Von Rad, Gerhard, *The Message of the Prophets*. Harper and Row, New York: 1965.

2. Brunner, Emil, *Revelation and Reason*. Westminster Press: 1996.

3. Keil, C. F. and Delitzsch, F., *Keil & Delitzsch Commentary on the Old Testament*. Peabody, Massachusetts: 1989. Vol. 11, [on Isaiah 2:3b] p 115.

4. Dunn, James F. G., *Did the First Christians Worship Jesus*? Westminster-John Knox Press, Louisville, Kentucky: 2010. p 116.

5. Robertson, A. T., *Word Pictures in the New Testament*. Broadman Press, Nashville, Tennessee: 1930. p 66

6. Von Rad, Ibid. p 66

7. Brown Driver Briggs, *Hebrew and English Lexicon*. Hendrickson Publishers Marketing, LLC, Peabody, Massachusetts: 2015. p.182.

8. K & D, Ibid. V.1, p 358.

9. Moody, Dale, *The Word of Truth*. Wm. B. Eerdmans, Grand Rapids, Michigan: 1981. p 40.

10. Eichrodt, Walter, *Theology of the Old Testament*, Vol 1, Westminster Press, Philadelphia, Pennsylvania: 1967. pp 69-80.

11. K & D, Ibid. V.1, Book 11, p 243.

12. Eichrodt, Ibid, p. 72

13. Von Rad, Ibid, p. 66, 72

14. Eichrodt, Ibid. p. 72, 80.

CHAPTER 2

15. Hort, F.J.A. *Judiatic Christianity*, Macmillan and Co: New York, 1894; p 2.

16. Eichrodt, Ibid p.64

17. Davidson, A. B., [9], TTOT on p. 58

18. Eichrodt, Ibid. p. 64

19. Von Rad, in TMOP, says on p. 148

20. Moody, Dale. TBBC, Vol. 10, p 238.

21. K & D, Ibid. Vol 1, p 71.

22. Moody, Dale Moody. *The Broadman Bible Commentary*, Broadman Press: Nashville, TN 1970, p 28.

23. Von RAD, Ibid.

24. K & D, Ibid. Vol. V111 p. 260.

25. K&D vol. 1 book 1; p 451

26. Foster, Richard. *Celebration of Discipline*, Harper: San Francisco, 1988, p 176

Chapter 3

27. K & D, Ibid, Vol. 11, Book 11, p 27.

28. Robertson. Ibid, WPONT Vol 11. P 25

29. Marshall, Alfred. *Parallel New Testament in Greek and English.* The Zondervan Corporation, Grand Rapids, MI 1990.

30. Von Rad, Ibid. TMOP, p 31

31. Davidson, Ibid. TTOT, p 82.

32. Augsburg confession: For more info on this confession of faith see -- (https://www.britannica.com/topic/Augsburg-Confession)

33. K & D. Ibid, Vol. 1, book 11 p. 53

34. K & D. Ibid, Vol 11, book 11 on p. 171

35. Davidson, Ibid. p 293

36. Davidson, Ibid. p. 68, 41.

37. Eichroth, op. cit in Vol 1, p 191.

38. K & D.   op. cit.

39. K & D. Ibid, vol 3, p 234.

40. Von Rad, Ibid, p 68.

CHAPTER 4

41. K&D, Ibid. Vol 10, p 4.

42. Von Rad, Ibid. TMOP, p 256.

43. K&D, Ibid. Vol 10, p 398.

44. Von Rad, Ibid. TMOP, p 256

45. Bright, John. in AHOI on p. 224.

46. Foster, Ibid. TSOLW on p. 398.

47. Bonhoeffer, Dietrich, "Bonhoeffer" p 105.

48. Ibid

49. Von Rad, Ibid. p 110.

50. Marshall, Ibid p 29.

Chapter 5

51. K&D. Ibid, p 75.

52. K&d. Ibid, Vol 11, p 154.

53. K&d. Ibid, vol 11, book 2; p 486.

54. K&D. Ibid, vol 7 book 1; p 248

55. Kaseman Ernst, *Commentary on Romans*, Grand Rapids, Michigan. Wm. B. Eerdmans Publishing, 1980.

56. Robertson. Ibid. Vol 4; p 238.

57. K&D. Ibid. Vol 7 p 62.

58. K&D. Ibid. Vol 2 Book 1; p. 56-62

59. K&d. Ibid Vol 2 book 2; p 131.

60. K&D. Ibid. p. 62.

61. Kaseman. Ibid. p ____.

62. K&D. Ibid. Vol 7 Book II p 143

Chapter 6

63. K&D Ibid. Vol 7, book 2, p 174ff

Chapter 8

64. Von Rad. Ibid. p 189.

65. Von Rad. Ibid. p 12

66. K&D. Ibid vol 10 book 11 p 188.

Chapter 10

67.   Robertson. Ibid. vol 4. P 334 ff.

68. Robertson. Ibid. vol 4 p 194.

69. Robertson. Ibid vol 4. P 505.

70. Von Rad. Ibid p 269.

Chapter 11

71. K&D. Ibid vol 6 p 278

72. K&D. Ibid vol 6 p. 301.

73. Septuagint [LXX] [Found in the NASB Introduction of Ecclesiastes], p 920 _____

74. Von Rad. Ibid. p 68.

75. K&D. Ibid vol 9 book 11 p 407.

Chapter 12

76. Von Rad. Ibid. p 256.

77. Ibid.

Chapter 13

78. was 84.   Robertson. Ibid WPOTNT, vol. 111. p 66.

79. Solman, S. D. F., ed. *The Expositor's Greek New Testament*: Vol 111; p 369.

80. Robertson. Ibid. Vol 11; p X111.

81. Ibid. p 10

82. Ibid. vol 11; p 15.

83. Ibid. p.7.

84. Ibid. vol 11. P 71.

Chapter 14

85. Robertson. Ibid. p 373.

86. Ibid p.74.

87. ibid. p. 72.

Chapter 15

88. Ibid. p 25.

89. Solmon. Ibid. p 388.

90. Abbot, . *Abbot's Commentary on Romans*. P 776. (Quote by Markus Barth).

91. Solmon, Ibid.

Chapter 16

92. Robertson. Ibid. vol 5 p.1.

Chapter 17

93. Robertson. Ibid. vol 111, p234.

94. Robertson. Ibid. vol 4 , p 476.

_____